A New York Memoir

Books by Richard Goodman

French Dirt: The Story of a Garden in the South of France

The Soul of Creative Writing

A New York Memoir

A New York Memoir

Richard Goodman

Transaction Publishers
New Brunswick (U.S.A.) and London (U.K.)

Second printing 2011
Copyright © 2011 by Transaction Publishers, New Brunswick, New Jersey.

"Why I Live in New York City" was first published in *Pilgrimage*; "The Man in White" in the *Harvard Review*; "Elegy for an English Bike" in the *New York Times*; "A Big Wonderful Tree Falling Down" in *Ascent*; "Surrendering to Provence" in *Travelers' Tales Provence*; "Maine Journal" in *High Horse: Contemporary Writing by the MFA Faculty of Spalding University*; "The Bicycle Diaries" in the *Louisville Review*; "When I'm Sixty-Four" in the *Rambler*; "My Beautiful Ann" in *Conclave*; "The Ceiling Leak" in *Ascent*; "Appointment in Cortlandt" in the *New York Times*; "Take the 'A' Train" in *River Teeth*.

All rights reserved under International and Pan-American Copyright Conventions. No part of this book may be reproduced or transmitted in any form or by any means, electronic or mechanical, including photocopy, recording, or any information storage and retrieval system, without prior permission in writing from the publisher. All inquiries should be addressed to Transaction Publishers, Rutgers—The State University of New Jersey, 35 Berrue Circle, Piscataway, New Jersey 08854-8042. www.transactionpub.com

This book is printed on acid-free paper that meets the American National Standard for Permanence of Paper for Printed Library Materials.

Library of Congress Catalog Number: 2010024097
ISBN: 978-1-4128-1492-8
Printed in the United States of America

Library of Congress Cataloging-in-Publication Data

Goodman, Richard, 1945-
  New York memoir / Richard Goodman.
    p. cm.
  Includes bibliographical references and index.
  ISBN 978-1-4128-1492-8 (alk. paper)
    1. New York (N.Y.)--Description and travel. 2. New York (N.Y.)--Social life and customs. 3. City and town life--New York (State)--New York. 4. Goodman, Richard, 1945- 5. Goodman, Richard, 1945---Homes and haunts--New York (State)--New York. 6. New York (N.Y.)--Biography. I. Title.

F128.55.G65 2010
974.7'1--dc22

2010024097

To my daughter

"No one should come to New York to live unless he is willing to be lucky."—E. B. White, *Here is New York*

Contents

Acknowledgements	ix
Introduction	xi
Why I Live in New York City	1
The Man in White	7
Leaving Soho	17
Elegy for an English Bike	21
A Big Wonderful Tree Falling Down	23
Surrendering to Provence	43
Maine Journal	49
The Bicycle Diaries	59
When I'm Sixty-Four	71
My Beautiful Ann	75
The Ceiling Leak	89
Appointment in Cortlandt	95
Take the "A" Train	103
The Wheaton Girl	111

Acknowledgements

Once again, I want to thank Sena Naslund and my colleagues at the MFA in Writing Program at Spalding University. Deborah Attoinese, insightful and fearlessly truthful as always, was a steady guiding beacon. Rick Moranis has been unstintingly generous in his counsel and direction. Every writer should have friends and steadfast encouragers like these.

I very much want to thank Irving Horowitz and Mary Curtis of Transaction Publishers for having faith in my book. I want to thank my editor, Larry Mintz, for his trusted opinions and guidance. And Mindy Waizer for her enthusiasm about my work.

I also want to thank, as always, my sister, Mary Downs, for her belief in me. That has never changed. That is true of Jo Boufford's support as well. Jody Lisberger deserves my gratitude for suggesting I bring these true stories together under a single roof. I want to thank Rebecca Walker for her unflagging support and wisdom. And I'm grateful for Eddie Lueken's encouragement when I really needed it. Thanks, too, to Molly Peacock, Bob Finch, Elaine Orr, and Kaylene Johnson for putting up with my title angst and calming me with excellent advice.

I want to thank the people I write about, some of whom are no longer here; I hope they can hear my gratitude: Edmond Landrier, Lavinia Russ, Iggy Keuchenius, Brenda Bowen, Ann Silberling, and, especially, my mother, Marianna Rehling. I have dedicated this book to my daughter, Becky. She is a character as a young girl in one of these stories, and I hope something approaching her bright spirit and big heart flows through this book.

Introduction

I came to New York City at the age of thirty, still homeless. That is, I'd never felt that I was at home in any of the places I lived. Not in Detroit, not in Chicago, not in Cambridge, Massachusetts. After a few weeks in New York, I did. I knew I was home. I've lived here contentedly for thirty years now.

Most of the stories in this book take place here; those that do not are highly influenced by New York. (The second story takes place in Cambridge, for example, my stepping stone to New York.) This is where I have grown old. Well, older. This is where I have fallen in love three times, where I have married, had a daughter, divorced, helped raise my daughter, and become a writer. I have done brave things here and cowardly things. I have shown the best in me and the worst in me. I have become who I am.

All of this has happened against the backdrop of a massive city of unmatchable energy and of sheer, brute authority. It is a city that is accepting and pitiless and inspiring. I believe in it, and I'm grateful for having lived here. I have seen it change radically in the thirty years I've lived here. I've seen it rich and freewheeling, and I've seen it fall on hard times and almost collapse. I've seen it grievously wounded, and I've seen it rehabilitate itself with the help of the entire world and with its own limitless moxie. It is just as much a character in this book as any of the people I write about who I have met here. And what I write about is love, loss, friendship, work, and death. It is a life on the pages you have here. It is time—my time—precious and rationed.

I call this book a memoir, because that's what it is. These fourteen true stories constitute an emotional chronicle with a single unmistakable setting.

Every one of us lives a life we did not expect to live. We begin with passions and dreams and with the basic conviction that all will turn out for the good, more or less. Some of it does turn out for the good. Most of it, though, is a startling combination of the unexpected and the inconceivable. Every door we walk through introduces us to a strange land, and then we set about seeing if this is a place where we can grow.

For me, New York City has been the great opened door.

Why I Live in New York City

You wake up next to a raven-haired woman who you love. You're in your apartment, which is on the second floor, facing East Tenth Street. The windows are long and tall, and have that opaque irregularity windows have that are a century old. Outside it's snowing. The flakes ease down languidly, like thousands of tiny parachutists. It's Saturday. The year is 1975. You are twenty-seven. You hold her body next to yours, brush your hand across her thigh. It trembles slightly. You rise and go to the small, arced fireplace in the living room and light the paper to a fire you prepared the night before. The paper erupts and soon there are hot swaying flames and the snap of splintered wood catching fire.

This is Tenth Street in the East Village, an astonishingly beautiful street, and you are lucky to be living here. How in God's name did you get the courage to come to this city? You remember those first few weeks after you arrived. How scared you were. You walked out of the Port Authority Bus Terminal smack into a mass of the most furious tidal wave of humanity you'd ever seen, and not one eye caught yours. The immensity of the place made you cower like a six year old. Your instinct was to turn around and go back home, and you almost did. So, why didn't you?

Because you were in a small town in Michigan, and everything you said was a lie. You betrayed yourself hourly. You disguised your yearnings well, but the problem was that you were wasting away. In order to survive, you felt you had to neuter your soul. Like those first moments when someone is shot in the spine, and the feeling begins to drain from the body progressively upward, so you felt your soul disappear progressively until you wondered if there was any of it left.

So you fled. It felt like you'd taken the last helicopter out of Saigon, that one perched on the embassy roof with the line of people trailing upward. You just made it, one of the last to climb the ladder before the doors shut and the chopper rose and angled away. You know it would have been death to stay, because you went back years later, and all the people you know were just finishing the sentences they began the moment you left. You had a brief year in Cambridge, with a few wonderful months learning to cook from a French chef, but that ended. Then it was time to swallow your fear and to come to New York.

So here you are in a building that is 150 years old that was a hospital in the Civil War. You have a girl you love, with raven rich hair, and firm legs and arms that encircle your neck and lips that kiss you firmly. She laughs at things you say with explosions of glee and sometimes bends over in pain you make her laugh so hard. It's Saturday. All day long.

You are walking on Greene Street in Soho, that strange, marvelous neighborhood populated by cast iron buildings as breathtaking as anything ever built in America. It is 7:30 on a summer evening. The air is soft. It is a twilight city light in which even steel seems benign. The street itself is made of bullion-shaped cobblestones. Despite their shiny solidness, they look vulnerable, because they were put there by hand, one by one, so many years ago. Many of the buildings you walk by have short iron loading docks and big doors and sooty windows. It is 1980.

Did you ever think that architecture would get into you this deeply, as deeply as painting and music? Now you know you are inspired by these cast iron buildings that have somewhere a spiritual affinity to Florence, by the simple grace of brownstones, by the great Brooklyn Bridge, the longest poem in the world, and by the rust-colored nineteenth-century brick warehouses looming near the Hudson River.

You arrive at 55 Greene Street. You shout up to a window. The window opens, a head emerges, and a key is thrown down to you. You open a gate-wide door and climb wooden creaking stairs. You are a young writer here to meet other writers and to work with them.

A door to the loft opens and you shyly—but not too shyly—enter. There they are. There are four women and six men. One of the women is named Chloe, full of betrayal you will find, and heartless. She has lynx eyes that bore through you and Veronica Lake hair, one wing of which flows over one side of her face. She has a feral baritone voice and the fullest, softest lips you've ever seen, and what a writer she is. You will fall so hard for her that she will repossess that soul you thought you got back, and absolutely nothing will be left, not even a sign saying "Formerly a Soul Resided Here." And you won't mind, that's how far gone you'll be.

She's from Texas. The second woman is from California, the third from Louisiana, and the fourth from Chicago. Three of the men are from California, one is from Alabama and one is from here. And you.

The owner of the loft has an unfiltered cigarette in his mouth. The smoke dragon-streams from his nostrils luxuriously. His has a small glass of whiskey at his side from which he sips from time to time. Will you ever possibly be as suave a writer as he is? Should you take up smoking unfiltered cigarettes and drinking whiskey, both of which you can't stand? Maybe you can try it at home, when you're alone, and see how it works. His girlfriend is here, too, straight-backed, tall, with luxurious supple hair in a thick Frieda Kahlo braid hanging behind her back. You fall in love with her, too, but so does every other man in the group.

All of you are here trying hard to write and to be true to what it is you need to say, and for the next eight years these people will champion your efforts and you theirs. This is your writer's group in Soho.

It is a sweltering summer in August. Everyone with any sense has abandoned the city. Not you, though. You not only stay, you like it. It's difficult to romanticize three-day-old garbage in August heat. Still, you're not appalled by the scent. Far from it. You think that if someone hasn't spent a sweltering summer here then they will never know it completely.

You are living in the East Village. It is 1985. The hot air sucks the breath out of you, and hits you in the stomach. The heat is so fierce you have oasis shimmers in the back of your eyes, and you walk like a man with terminal heart disease. It is so hot you have to be careful about touching street lamps. You are sitting on a stoop of a brownstone apartment next to people who live there. Some you know, some you don't. The heat has forced you all out on the street. You are living in Elmer Rice's city and in Weegee's city and in Henry Roth's city, a world you love, of ordinary people from another era. There you all are, men and women, some younger, some older, all depleted from the heat, the women struggling against the despot of modesty, the men in armless T-shirts, or bare above the waist.

You see pretty young women, normally vigilant about buttoned blouses and the high-water mark of skirts when they sit. They abandon all decorum. They have hair that sticks to sweaty necks, and the backs of the blouses are damp and flat against their back and the high backs of their skirts are damp and even the inside of their thighs, showing wonderful maps of desire, and so many blouse buttons are unbuttoned you believe in Santa Claus again. And when they sit on the stoops they pull their skirts up high for any possible breeze, and this approaches the total sheet-discarding indifference of childbirth.

Here on this stoop in the heat you encounter the oral tradition of storytelling from these urban *griots*. In the sultry evening, you listen to the man who went to parties where Kerouac sat on a couch and Ginsberg was there as well as Corso. What did they say, you ask? What where they like? You listen to the aged black superintendent who proudly says he saw Joe Lewis knock out Max Schmelling. And you say, you mean you were in there? And he says, yes I was. And someone heard Emma Goldman speak once, in Union Square. You don't know who Emma Goldman was yet, but you nod appreciatively. Here, everyone is a storyteller, and that's what you want to be, too. You are part of this oral tradition now, and the storytellers have cans of Schaefer beer and panting dogs and cigarettes glowing in the late evening, and you could listen all night, all night long.

This city is powered by dreams, wide-awake dreams that don't vanish with the dawn but that stay vibrant all day and night. These dreams give off a Blakean light, like those arrows of desire. The place is charged with them. The dreamers are odd types, but inside the strangely dressed figures with the irregular habits and ambiguous personalities is that most unstable of emotions on the periodic table, hope. Despite how hard it can be to simply survive here and how coldly dismissive and indifferent the city can be, it will somehow and always encourage that hope with a soft breath on the embers. Just when you are ready to admit your dream extinguished, it pulses with new heat and could at any minute become a conflagration.

God, what a mess this place is, a hot stinking crowded rude impossible arrogant mess. You need to get out before you start smashing car windows and screaming at hobbling senior citizens who take too long to get on the bus. But where will you go to forge in the smithy of your soul what desperately needs to be forged? Who will encourage the fire that never has died, and never will? Who will embrace you as indifferently and as fully? There is always a time to leave, and one day you will. But not yet. For now, you'll stay here in New York, that great impossible understander.

The Man in White

In 1975, I was thirty years old, living in Cambridge, Massachusetts, and fairly miserable. I was at loose ends, in one of those becalmed times we have in our lives, not knowing what I wanted to do. I hated Cambridge. Maybe that was because I was working at the Spaghetti Emporium as a waiter. The Spaghetti Emporium was, how shall I put it, a cavernous restaurant in a basement off Harvard Square that served fourth-rate food—spaghetti, obviously, with various uninspired sauces—in dingy, clamoring surroundings to a highly demanding clientele.

The restaurant was cheap in every way you can imagine, but the most inventive way was with entertainment. There wasn't much of it, but one night we had a singer. He was a singer of popular Italian street songs—you know, *O Sole Mio,* that sort of thing. He was nine years old. He showed up with his mother. He was dressed in a blue tuxedo with elaborate ruffles and shiny patent leather shoes. A fellow waiter and I looked incredulously as he started to croon—for that's exactly what he did. The sound system was hardly functioning, and acoustics were from the Lascaux caves. After two songs, the boy had unfastened his bow tie and opened the top two buttons of his shirt, Dean Martin-style. When he knelt down before an octogenarian female diner, looked into her eyes, and warbled, "That's amore!" I vowed to do something else with my life.

But what? I had a master's degree in English, but I couldn't get a teaching job in one day, or even in one month. Besides, this town was full of aimless young men and women with multiple degrees standing on corners ready to teach. Should I get yet another waiting job? The thought made me retch. I had thought seriously about moving to New York City, had dreamed of it, but I didn't have the gumption—yet.

I lived on Gray Street, not terribly far from Harvard Square, and every day I walked to work. I found a shortcut that would take me through a little alley past a small French restaurant called Chez Jean and onto Shepard Street. From there, I walked past the Commons to my dreaded job. My shift at the Spaghetti Emporium started at 4, so I would begin my walk early from Gray Street. I liked to take my time and enjoy the last few moments of freedom and fresh air. I remember the time of year was late spring, and the trees were in full bloom. When I walked down the little alleyway, I would see the open back door of Chez Jean, leaving just a screen door between me and whatever was within. I would see a shadowy figure from time to time moving across the entranceway, obscured somewhat by the screen door's mesh. Who was that, I wondered.

But what really enthralled me were the smells coming out of that back door and floating into my nose and brain. They were rich, deep, complex, and intense. They were new to me. I couldn't tell what they were, but whatever they were, I was their slave for the half minute it took me to walk past that open door. So delicious! I could smell skill, care, and subtlety in the air. Then I'd be past Chez Jean and back into the real world, walking to work.

The day after the infamous boy singer episode, his prepubescent voice still ringing in my ear, I got ready, once again, to make my way to the Spaghetti Emporium. I had it in my mind that I was going to get out, but I was stumped as to how. I walked from my apartment and turned down the alleyway to walk by Chez Jean. It was a splendid day, balmy and fragrant. The back door was open. The gorgeous smells came to me, once again.

Instead of passing by, I stopped. I walked to the screen door. I opened it. And I walked in.

Suddenly, as if I had walked through the wardrobe in the *Chronicles of Narnia*, I was in a different world. I was in a natural-light-infused kitchen. The room had a high ceiling, at the top of which were two broad skylights. It was quiet in there, I noticed right away. There was a massive gas stove, heavy and formidable looking. On it, two giant pots stood with the barest flicker under them. I could see they were each filled to the brim with a bouillon-like concoction, percolating slowly away, with the skins of onions and tomatoes and portions of celery stalks and carrot ends on the surface. My nose told me that this was the source of some of the wonderful smells that had enthralled me every day as I walked by.

I was taking all this in with wonder. But here was a man in front of me, dressed in white fatigues with a long white apron. He had a russet moustache and somewhat weary eyes, and an expression of deep curiosity on his face.

"Yes, may I 'elp you?" he said in an accent that seemed to me unmistakably French.

"I...I..." and here all those harried, greasy, plate-banging evenings at the Emporium gave me the motivation I needed.

"I...I want a job!" I said much louder than normal. "I want to learn to cook! I want to be a chef! I want to learn French!"

He blinked. The thing of it was, he hardly reacted to this disturbed individual in his kitchen with flailing arms. He simply said, "Do you 'ave any 'xperience?"

"No!" I said with great conviction, as if this were the one supreme skill any employer would desire in a worker.

"Oh," he said. Then he rubbed his chin. "Well, it 'appens that my assistant go to a hospital yesterday to have his appendix taken out. Now I am without an assistant."

"Great!" I said. *"Take me!"*

"You are available?"

"Yes! All I have to do is quit my job. I can do that right now."

"Well, then, ok."

"What? Really?"

"Ok. Yes."

"Thank you! *Merci!*" I said.

I introduced myself. The man in white before me said his name was Edmond Landrier. We shook hands. His grip was strong. I could see his rope-thick forearm muscles working. He gave me a basic tour of the kitchen and explained how things went, but it was all a blur. He told me the hours, and we discussed money, but I would probably have worked for nothing. I said goodbye and walked out of the back door I had so recently walked through.

My life had changed in an instant. I strolled to the Emporium, whistling, and quit my job.

The next day, I returned at the appointed hour of 2 PM. Edmond got me outfitted into some whites and an apron. I felt like I had been transformed. What now? I stood there in my unblemished whites, ignorant as a spoon, waiting. First, I had to become acquainted with everything in the kitchen. Edmond opened a large refrigerator.

"'Ere you 'ave the butter, the parsley, the terrine."

"What's a terrine?" I said.

He looked at me quizzically. "This." He pulled out an oval-shaped dish full of pâté, except it wasn't smooth.

"Oh, you mean pâté."

"No. Terrine. This is pâté." He showed me another oval dish with a silky smooth surface.

And so on, throughout the kitchen, showing me all the instruments of cooking—pots, pans, ladles, and so on, all larger than life. He showed me the sharpest knives I'd ever seen. I say "seen," because they were so sharp, they shimmered, sending out waves of allure, drawing me toward them, like sirens, seeming to say, "Come here. With your finger. One day, you'll be ours."

I looked at Edmond as he explained the kitchen to me. He was a sinewy, medium-sized man who looked fatigued, and undoubtedly was. His face seemed to glisten with a light film of sweat. He had a habit of punctuating his talk by sniffing, which would raise one end of his moustache as if it were winking. His eyes were bloodshot. His voice was a baritone, perfect for speaking French, or for speaking French-accented English. He didn't talk much, though, but when he did, I listened raptly.

After the tour, he began his prep work for the evening with me standing by his side. There were a slew of things to do in a specific order that never changed. Ducks had to be roasted. Sauces had to be made. Rice had to be baked—yes, baked. Parsley had to be chopped fine and then squeezed of its juice to be used as garnish. Stock had to be poured through cheesecloth into containers and cooled. Apple tarts had to be made and cooked. I was trying to take it all in, writing down things furiously in a little notebook I brought with me. I was overwhelmed. I continued to be overwhelmed for the next few weeks.

When he talked about cooking, Edmond was direct and unambiguous. When I did something wrong—which, at the beginning, was constantly—he simply said, "That is not the way to do it." He never qualified that. Even if what I did was just marginally wrong, Edmond still said, "That is not the way to do it." He was even-tempered, mostly, and only barked at me a few times in the six months I worked for him.

I learned that Edmond had grown up in the Jura region of France, which is mountainous and often snowy, and not far from Switzerland. He apprenticed as a cook when he was fifteen. When he was eighteen, he went into the army and was sent to Algeria during that difficult war. Once he said to me, "I 'ave even eaten camel." He spoke little about the past. It didn't interest him. He was married to a French-Canadian woman, and they had no children. He took his vacations in Canada, and he liked nothing better than going to a remote lake and fishing and then sitting on the porch of a rented cabin and drinking beer as he watched the sunset. He laughed infrequently, but he did have a sense of humor. Once I asked him if he ever cooked for his family when he lived in France. "Yes, but I use up every pot and pan in the 'ouse—and they never ask me to cook again!" He smiled broadly at that story.

Edmond had originally been a pastry chef. That was his formal training in France. When he came to Boston, he found that he couldn't make a living simply as a pastry chef, so he learned to cook everything else on the menu. But he was still a pastry chef at heart. I remember standing next to him as he showed me how to make an apple tart. "What's a tart?" I asked. Again, I got that quizzical look, this time with a sniff and the raised moustache. I watched as he mixed flour with butter in a bowl. He never looked directly at me but spoke toward the bowl as he mixed the flour and butter into a double-fist-sized ball. He talked to me of how dough behaved and how to manage it. I had never heard anyone talk about an ingredient this way. He took a rolling pin. "You put some flour. *Pas trop.* Not too much." In a motion as if he were tossing seeds to birds, he sprinkled the surface of the table with flour and sprinkled the pin, too. He took the rolling pin and, using the flats of his outstretched palms to maneuver the center of the pin, he began to urge the ball of dough outward.

"You don't use the handles?" I asked.

"No. I 'ave more control this way."

And it was true! I saw how the dough obeyed Edmond, splaying outward in perfect measures, this way and that, to a uniform thickness, guided by only the pressure of his palms on the center of the rolling pin. He made deft, small adjustments, pressing slightly on the center of the pin with one palm and then with another. When the dough was rolled out, he took two fingers and slid them under the pale, flaccid blanket. "You see it is all the same thickness," he said, holding part of it up for me to see. It looked easy, but God save me, it was not. I learned later how hard it was to use a rolling pin gracefully.

Edmond used a knife to cut the dough into a slim rectangular shape, the basic form of a tart. His fingers manipulated the sides of the dough, making swift surgical pinches, first on one side, then the other. This produced a fluted border that, when baked, looked very pretty indeed. He cut another slim rectangle from the remaining dough.

"Now you try," he said.

I pinched the sides of dough in what I thought was a similar motion as Edmond's. The results looked as if I were trying to harm the dough.

"That is not the way to do it," Edmond said. He showed me again. It took me four weeks to learn to maneuver dough well enough for Edmond to give me his highest approval: "That is ok." When he did, I felt like I'd done something heroic.

Edmond showed me how to do the simplest things, the most basic things—like chopping an onion and slicing a carrot in the French way. This consisted of cutting the onion first vertically, then horizontally, and then vertically once again, which produced small, perfect cubes. That was surprisingly difficult. This was mainly because the difference between doing this at home and doing it for money in a restaurant is *speed.* At home, you can work at your leisure. There is too much to do in too little time in a restaurant. Edmond took a knife. It bristled with sharpness, nearly hissing at me. He wore his white kitchen shirt with the top two buttons open, showing me some wan, glistening skin. He first showed me how to chop an onion, everything going so fast as if his hand were programmed. Then he showed me how to slice a carrot into perfect, blunt juliennes. He asked me to try. Thankfully, he walked away to work on something else.

I peeled eight or nine carrots. A peeled carrot is wet and slippery, and, most challenging, round. It's very hard to maintain with your fingers. I had to first cut the carrot in half. I grasped the recalcitrant carrot with my fingertips as Edmond had showed me. I picked up the heavy, sharp knife, but the carrot slithered out of my grasp before I could cut it. I tried again, but this time the carrot sprung from my grip and shot off the table. Edmond, who always seemed to see my mistakes even with his back turned, came over.

"That is not the way to do it," he said. He took the knife from my hand and held the carrot firmly with the tips of his fingers and then cut the carrot cleanly in half with a perfect incision. He gave me the knife. "You must be the boss of the carrot," he said. "You must not let the carrot be the boss of you."

Becoming the boss of the carrot proved difficult. That's when the awaiting knife finally made its move and sliced through my thumbnail without even a whisper. The knife was so sharp I didn't even feel what happened. Then I noticed my carrot was drizzled with blood. Edmond fetched a small first aid kit from a cabinet and took out a few band aids. "'Ere," he said, handing them to me. It was about then that the thumb began to throb, as if it contained my heart. The knife had been the boss of me.

As the tart baked, as the ducks roasted, as the stock bubbled slowly away, as the *coq au vin* cooked, the kitchen slowly filled with those magnificent smells that had ravished me on my walks by the back door. Those rich, deep, complex, and intense smells. All in the light-filled stillness of a warm summer afternoon. This time, though, I was helping in their creation. This was perhaps the first time I was conscious of the rigors of trying to attain perfection. This was exciting beyond telling.

What I am leaving out, of course, is the actual cooking for the actual patrons. I wanted to give you an impression of my slow emergence out of ignorance first, and what is was like to learn from Edmond Landrier. The restaurant opened its doors at six o'clock. Before that, the three or four waiters who worked at Chez Jean would arrive and begin setting up their stations. Oh, how glad I was I wasn't one of them! Never mind the restaurant was so much better than the Spaghetti Emporium. It was the idea that now I was in the kitchen, making and creating—and *not* a waiter. Then the dishwasher arrived, and the French woman who seated people and took reservations came with her hauteur. Edmond and I would banter with them a bit, but we didn't have much free time. We were prepping right up until the first order was placed.

The pace picked up gradually, quarter hour by quarter hour, until, at 8 o'clock, it was at its absolute height. That's when the place became slightly anarchic and desperate. At its furious height, the kitchen was broiling hot—hot as a windowless tool shed on a scorching July day. I was constantly behind, trying to make up for lost time, and this inevitably made me make mistakes in my rush. Edmond, though, no matter how harried he got, was able to salvage things, adjusting matters here and there to compensate for my overzealousness. Still, it could get like that famous scene in Charlie Chaplin's *Modern Times* where it's impossible for the Little Tramp to keep up with the assembly line. Pressure, pressure, pressure. Tempers flared. Patrons wanted to know where their food was. Edmond, angry that they didn't understand this was a French restaurant and that dishes were made to order and not pre-prepared, would say, "Well, why don't you tell them to get a *Beeg* Mac?" Somehow we got through it.

I burned myself on a regular basis. It was impossible not to. Pots and pans had to be moved hurriedly, and dishes had to be taken out of the furiously hot oven. When you reach for a pot or a pan on a stove in a harried kitchen, without looking carefully, you don't think about where the handle's been. It may have been over a flame—this was a gas stove, remember. That handle might be nebula-hot. When you reach inside an oven to snatch out a pan, your forearm will more often than not touch a scorching oven rack. Once I burned a wide, translucent path on my forearm. "Look at this!" I said to Edmond. He smiled a small smile. Then he rolled up his sleeve and showed me seventeen or eighteen permanent stripes on his arm, one after another, from his wrist to his biceps, looking like some kind of bizarre rank. Then he rolled down his sleeve. "Oh," I said.

From time to time I would be so hot and depleted, I had to walk outside, out that celebrated screen door, to take desperate breaths of fresh, soft night air. It was almost as if I were drowning in heat inside. I was so grateful to breathe in this outside air. I couldn't stay long. Just a minute or two was lovely.

At the end of the evening, when we had finished cooking and had cleaned the stove and swept the floor and put everything away, Edmond went to the basement refrigerator and got two cold beers, one for each of us. This was the most honest, satisfying beer I've ever drank, and it went down, cold swig and after cold swig, like a delicious dream. Then, around eleven at night, out of my war-worn whites and back into my own clothes, I'd walk the two or three minutes back to my apartment where I would shower and collapse into my bed, spent.

The next morning I'd wake up gradually, but by two o'clock, I was ready to do it all over again.

Then there was the actual moment, like learning a new language, when I shifted from ignorance into some form of workable knowledge. When I was actually more of an asset than a liability—when I was a cook. And one day, Edmond—and I don't remember what prompted this—stopped what he was doing in the kitchen and said to me, "I think you are learning how to cook." This I still think about today, so many years later.

In six months, Edmond Landrier took a raw recruit, a young man who didn't know his head from his aspic, to a level of acceptable competency in a French kitchen. That is not to say that I was ready to open my own French bistro in New York, but it is to say that I knew how to make a proper terrine, a good *tarte au pomme*, and a *sauce basquaise*; I knew how to create a *sauce béarnaise*, a veal Marengo, and *riz de veau*. I knew how to chop and slice onions, carrots, and parsley in the French style, proficiently and rapidly. I knew how to make a savory *coq au vin*, how to make five or six crêpes Suzettes in a flash, how to turn out a good-looking *sole amandine*. I knew how to make stocks, cook tomatoes Provençal, how to sauté, roast, and bake.

I learned that failure in a French kitchen can often be declared a victory with a little bit of magic, and so I must never despair. I learned how to be graceful under pressure, how to stand up for myself, how to never be satisfied with the imperfect, the less-than-right, the ill-made. I learned economy, how nothing was ever wasted in a French kitchen, and that we can exist and succeed with less.

And I could do it all in the blistering heat of an excited, harried kitchen at its peak on a hot Saturday evening in July.

Then, almost as mysteriously as it had begun, I had to walk back out the door again, for good. The restaurant closed for all of July and August, and I would need to find another job. I knew it was time for a bigger leap than those that I had made before, and so I decided to move away from Cambridge—to New York City. I was ready. I had the gumption I lacked months earlier. My life would take an entirely different course after that. But I'd never forget those months in the heat of the kitchen. I'd never forget what I learned by walking through that magical back door, one desperate spring afternoon, from Edmond Landrier, the man in white.

Leaving Soho

Soho bestowed the gift of loneliness on me E.B. White speaks of during the summer of 1980, and I am still grateful. From March through the end of August of that year, I lived on Crosby Street in New York City's Soho, one of the least transformed streets in this strange artistic-industrial area. I was getting over a broken relationship, a five-year co-habitation that was, essentially, a marriage. Soho is where I went to sort out my heart and mind and to experience the many small and large devastations that come with a broken love affair.

Soho had great charm then, and, despite the colossal changes that have taken place there, it does still. I found that many of its unique characteristics served me well in my period of convalescence. The first of these was, simply, that not many people lived there thirty years ago. When the long lines of trucks left the sides of the streets in the afternoon, and the art speculators and tourists fled with them, not many personalities were left. For such a large area—even speaking of so many years ago, I am excluding weekends—it was sparsely populated. So that often I could be quite alone with my loneliness, free to roam from street to street in near or even complete solitude, feeling my melancholy nurtured by silence and space. Hearing my own footsteps clack and clomp in loud singularity during an evening stroll was often antidote enough for some feeling of wrack that suddenly overtook me. And it helped, at times, to feel my hurt was the only hurt around, and Soho let me feel that easily.

In particular, this was true of my street, Crosby Street, with its empty longitudinal expanse and its rough cobblestones. At times, there was literally no one walking or driving down this street for close to an hour. I would stand outside my building and communicate with this emptiness. I could sigh deeply, as the heartsick are wont to do, and Crosby Street, with great beneficence, ingested my woe, accepted it, seemed to request more. It was constant in its willingness, a big, loyal, mute friend that was always there when I came home alone. I felt especially tender toward the cobblestones. They seemed to me, even in their density, a sort of delicate and vulnerable touch within the context of all this cast iron strength. There were not a few days when I spoke mentally to these cobblestones which had so obviously been planted by human hands, and I felt very protective toward them.

Soho's sparseness also had the simple but startling effect of granting a lot more attention to individuals. This was an incomparable gift. It was not unusual, for example, to see a single person walking on the opposite side of the street, making it just you and him or her, strolling for minutes along together on opposite sides, the only humans around in all this real estate. I never saw people more clearly, more distinctly than in Soho. That meant much to me. It was a form of human contact that was almost intimate—it was certainly private in one respect—and if I didn't actually meet the person walking toward me and then by me, I did feel there was an exchange nevertheless. I can still remember faces and nods and hellos and unabashed eye contact. This contact was my first tentative reaching out for closeness again.

Because there were so few people in Soho then, each person, as I said, became dramatically unique in your eyes. This was particularly wonderful with women. Soho had—has, still, if you are observant—beautiful women, healthy, energetic, and alluring. There were times when I was more grateful for that than for anything else. The women I saw were often dramatically highlighted as they passed by stark industrial facades and closed diners and empty street corners. I could gaze at them for minutes instead of seconds as is the case uptown, follow them and their colors and clothes coming toward me, and even begin a smile almost a block away. It's hard to imagine that occurring in Soho today. And they were generous with their smiles! I can remember a pair of eyes, the way a dress clung to a stomach, lovely legs, the way a woman turned a corner and was off. I had four months of this display, and though at times it made me ache with wanting, it also made me feel vibrant and cheery and full of awe. Those were feelings I sorely needed after leaving a relationship that had left me numb and cold.

Another of Soho's particularities that helped me gently through the spring was its weather. Because Soho is a separate commonwealth of sorts—I think its architecture has a great deal to do with this—it seems to have its own weather. This is singularly true of rain. A rainstorm in Soho can have as much significance and drama as it does on an island. During that particular spring there were three or four very violent rainstorms, and experiencing them in Soho was restorative. A rain in Soho always brought out a childlike feeling in me. As the water came washing down with pulsing force, I sat in my small loft, huddled with my yellow lamps in the cool humid obscurity, enjoying every noisy minute of it. I would leave the windows open and thrill to the loud rain and occasional spritzing I got as the wind blew some of the storm into my room. The thunder crashed and rumbled, and I felt an exquisite blanket of innocence and youth and openheartedness as it rained and rained and rained.

There were other attractions. Like playing basketball at Spring and Thompson on the small court where local Italian-American kids took up sides. They still do, thank heavens. Or the adjacent playground where I used to come after work and watch children play. And the gigantic R & K Bakery on Prince near West Broadway, defunct now, which was one of the biggest—if not the biggest in the city. "One day you're the biggest, the next day someone else is," a worker once told me. By necessity, it was a nocturnal operation. I remember going out walking at 2 AM and coming upon four or five men in wrinkled whites sitting on a stoop taking a breather as the building heaved out its concentrated essences of fresh bread. That sugared wind snapped my olfactory senses wide awake.

There were a few special shops and stands, a favorite bar or two, perhaps, and bookstores. But though I liked these very much, every neighborhood can usually claim the same. It was, in the end, this superb gift of loneliness, couched in so restful, poetic, and accepting a manner that made living in Soho then so good, and made it so difficult to leave. Soho had been with me in my time of need. For four brief months I shared with it everything I had, and it said, yes, all right, that's good. This kindness had its effect. Because when I finally did leave, I felt patched together not in some haphazard fashion, but that the job had been done well, smooth, strong, and seamless.

Elegy for an English Bike

My bicycle was stolen the other day. Or maybe I should say my friend was kidnapped on West 23rd Street sometime between 7 PM and 10 PM It was a Raleigh three-speed, English, heavy, black, and one of the most remarkable machines I've ever had. It was no effete, high-strung ten-speed from Italy or Japan. No, it was made of solid steel, rugged, not easy to carry, but a masterpiece. I feel a deep gloom without it.

It was made in the city of Nottingham in that most fastidious way we have come to associate with the best of things English. As with all such objects in which one can sense that something far deeper than just the maker's skill went into its creation, I felt a certain responsibility toward it and its well-being.

I got a sense of this Britannic sentiment simply by reading the owner's manual. On page 4, it says, "Before you begin any journey..." and goes on to present you with a safety checklist. What a lovely idea, to have a *journey* on a bicycle—and a proper word, indeed, if you see your bicycle as a kind of companion.

Its seat wasn't a seat; it was a saddle. And as such it was to be given particular care. Real, tough leather it was, precisely shaped, and I kept it in condition by applying a foul-smelling salve to its underside every so often. I felt obliged to do that.

Oh, but how well built this bicycle was! Its pedals, its gears, its brakes, everything about it was solid and worked flawlessly. People used to approach me when I was out with it and marvel at the gears or single-speed drive. "I ain't seen nothin' like that on a bicycle before," a Hell's Angel once told me as he peered intently at it.

"We—its manufacturers—are very proud of it," the manual states. I was proud of it. It had heft, and it was wonderfully balanced. But it was tough, too. I always felt supremely confident riding it, if one can ever feel confident riding a bicycle on the avenues of New York. Like the postman, I felt nothing could deter it from its appointed rounds.

I rode it almost exclusively in the city for the four or five years I owned it. During that time, it stood up to every malicious depression, every pothole, every declivity—not to mention several spontaneously opened car doors—that the borough threw at it. I rode it on the East Side, West Side, all around the town, in all states of weather and at all times. I rode it at dawn and past midnight, in rain, snow and in bursting sunshine. I rode it in heavy traffic and in Central Park with all the others and their reed-slim bicycles.

Sunday morning was the most exhilarating time to ride. I would take it out early, before the people emerged and clogged the thoroughfares. Downtown we'd glide, to TriBeCa and Soho—to an empty Soho, if you please. Then over to Chinatown or maybe to Henry Street for a sense of the immigrant past. How geography changed before my eyes on that bicycle! I can still remember the sense of utter freedom flying down some mild grade on a summer morning, banking around a deserted corner in TriBeCa, the majestic rusty warehouses looming overhead.

I feel as if I've lost a good friend. As the writer Henry Miller said about his bicycle, "Did it not see me through all my times of trouble and despair?" Yes. It did. I just hope the person who stole it has the decency to look after it.

It was superb.

A Big Wonderful Tree Falling Down

"Come *in*," she said, waving me in with a low hand. I caught the door, and she turned around in a measured pivot, giving me her back and talking as she walked toward the living room.

"I don't know why you want to see an old lady like me," she said as she hobbled away from me. I could see she was bent over. She had that smallish hump in her back many old people have, and it seemed to weigh on her heavily.

I laughed self-consciously. I didn't have a reply. I followed her, experiencing all the excitement, nervousness, and tension you feel when you give yourself over to a new person. I was being polite, too, trying to appear well bred. I wasn't sure how to do that in a brief walk from her foyer to her living room. I decided walking softly was the best way. I was also trying to take everything in. Her apartment was modest, but pleasant, though somewhat dark. The window in the living room faced to the back of her building, an unglamorous structure on Greenwich Village's Eight Street, between Fifth Avenue and Broadway.

"Sit. Sit," she said when we were both fully in the living room.

Her eyes flickered toward the only couch in the room. She sat in a tall dark chair behind her desk and immediately lit a cigarette.

"So, you're Mr. *Good*man," she said, as if by saying my name things could now begin.

"Yes, but please call me Richard."

"All right," she said. I waited for her to return the gesture. She didn't. She took a long drag from her cigarette and then tapped the stalk on the ashtray. Later, after I had visited her a few times, I asked her if I might call her by her first name, Lavinia.

"Of course!" she said. "Such a silly name, isn't it?"

"Well, no...."

"Oh, it *is*. It's Latin. The name of some third-rate Roman *goddess*. I think Mother had just read *Bullfinch's Mythology* when she had me. I've *never* liked my name."

Her full name was Lavinia Russ. Even now, when I put it down on paper, she emerges from the fog of time to greet me once again. Lavinia. La-vin-i-ah. A honey-sounding name.

"*They,*" she said, waving a hand somewhere, "they didn't say too much about you. But you look like a nice man."

At first, I had no idea what "they" she was talking about. I looked wildly in the direction of her extended hand for a clue. Suddenly, I realized that *they* were the Village Visiting Neighbors, a local nonprofit organization in New York City's Greenwich Village. They bring people together with older people who need errands done for them, or who simply want someone to visit them to quell the loneliness. It was *they* who had matched us together. In all the time I knew her, Lavinia never spoke the actual name of this organization. So, here I was. On my first visit.

"Well, I want to warn you," Lavinia said as she took a quick puff of her cigarette, "I'm losing my mind." She cast a half glance my way but avoided actually looking at me.

"Oh," I smiled, trying to think of something to say to counteract that.

"I can't re*mem*ber things anymore." She struggled with the words. "Words and names I used to be able to pluck out of the air at *will*. I find as I get older, I simply can't remember them."

"But that doesn't mean th...."

"I must be going...*what* do you call it when old people lose their memory?"

"Senile!" I said brightly.

"*Senile!* Yes. *Thank* you. Alec used to say—you don't know Alec, but he was a great friend of mine—he used to say, 'Lavinia, for God's sake, you never could remember those things *anyway.*'"

"But *I* forget things all the time, too. All the time!" I said.

"You do?" She sounded like she wanted to believe me, but she was tentative.

"Yes! I'm constantly forgetting things. I even forget what race I am."

This brought a deep rolling laugh from her. At its height, it was accompanied by, then evolved into, a wet smoker's cough, the kind that sounds alarmingly like splitting wood.

"No, really," I said, mildly alarmed at her cough but satisfied at my ability to make her laugh, "I'm not kidding. I *do* forget things."

"Well, that's awfully nice of you to say that, but I don't quite think it's the same thing." She stabbed her cigarette out, then immediately reached for another from a long lime-colored pack. "Old age," she snorted, as her hand trembled with the lighted match.

And so it was, old age. That and so many other things we talked about in the two years I knew Lavinia. Many, many things we discussed, but old age came back again and again and pushed its way to the front of the line, like a rude, bossy tourist, demanding to be served first. Now, some fifteen years later, as I approach the periphery of that harsh land myself, I think of those years, and of her, again and again.

As Lavinia talked, I stole glances at her, trying to drink in this new being, this fresh face. She had very pale, almost sallow skin. She had wrinkles, true, but not the deep Lillian Hellman-like slashes. Hers were thinner, and not as profound. I guessed she might be seventy-five. (It turned out she was eighty-one.) Yet she had the most vibrant hair. The color was an appealing blend of russet and wheat, with tinges of gray. It was cut fairly short and flowed in supple waves. It was rich, delicious.

Because her body was simply no longer up to it, her eyes, and, naturally, her voice, were the major ways in which Lavinia communicated her considerable variety of moods and emotions. Lavinia's eyes, though somewhat cloudy—she was eventually to have two cataract operations—were formidable. They could, and often did, in a single hour's time, definitively express surprise, remorse, sadness, anger—this occasionally, but what a fearsome sight!—skepticism and worry. I felt I always had to look at Lavinia's eyes, for fear of missing something dramatic and essential. In intimate partnership with those stagy eyes was a voice that was frayed and prone to fatigue but which, on any given day, could find its full measure and have you on the edge of your seat. Or, perhaps closer to the mark, could reach out and grab you by the scruff of the neck, as if you were a wanton cat. Just as it did now.

"The thing is," she burst out, "I don't *like* old people. I can't think of anything *worse* than sitting in a room with a bunch of old people." She shuddered. "They're always compl*ain*ing."

"And so you don't want to be like them?" I was cautious. I was leaving myself the option of retraction.

"No," she said, "I don't."

No, she didn't. She did everything in her power not to be jettisoned into that general bin labeled *old*. I'm sure that was one reason why she contacted Village Visiting Neighbors. It was to have some young blood flowing through her days.

"I mean," she continued, "have you seen those television commercials with that *what's-her-name* woman talking about diapers?"

She had stymied me. "Johnson and Johnson?" I said. I named a brand, because I had no idea what woman she was talking about.

"I don't *know*," Lavinia said, not hearing me correctly, "but she used to be in all those college musicals in the 40's. Small. A little too cute for me."

"Oh! You mean June Allyson!" My outburst about a somewhat obscure movie star sounded a bit too gay to me. I toned myself down. I suddenly knew what commercial she was talking about. It was for protective undergarments for old people.

"Yes! That's the one. And they even talk about in*con*tinence." She shuddered as if asked to eat something unspeakable.

I remembered the commercial well. All the while June Allyson, now aged and speaking huskily, her voice cracking—she no longer had that sweet sexual whisper from her earlier days in the movies—talked with a cheerful frankness about the "troubles" some old people have. *That needn't be,* she said. What sent a shiver flying down *my* back was the garment itself: large, plastic and elastic-banded. A king-sized diaper, really, that a two hundred-pounder could easily slip into.

"I wouldn't be caught *dead* wearing one of those," Lavinia said with bitterness in her voice. "I'd rather urinate in public. So humiliating!"

"Yes, I have to agr...."

"Now, dear," she said, ceremoniously placing her cigarette down on the ashtray, "I want to hear about *you*."

I blurted out a few things. Job: advertising copywriter. Marital status: single. Age: forty-five. And so on. As I tossed off this necessary but hollow-sounding data, I realized one of the things that was so exciting and yet bewildering about this, my first visit with Lavinia. The fact was that, aside from relatives, I didn't *know* any old people. True, I saw them in the street. I jostled up against them in lines. I watched them being picked up Sunday mornings to go visit their children and grandchildren. But I didn't have any friends who were over sixty.

"....of those advertisements on television are so clever. I adore those commercials with that man who sells *chickens*."

Lavinia startled me out of my reverie.

"Oh, you mean Frank Purdue."

"I don't know, but they're awfully clever."

"Yes, they are," I said. The truth was, my heart wasn't in my profession, the "craft" of advertising, as the insiders called it. Craft, my ass. But that was another story. "Did you know he act...."

"Now, dear, before you go." Lavinia had a short list in her hand, and she began speaking about it without looking at me. "If you can't get the peach, then any kind will do. And for this I need the small-sized carton—not the big one, *please*. The last person they sent couldn't manage to get that straight. And *here's* the money."

Was the visit at an end? I put my coat on and went out, and in a few minutes bought her what she needed from a delicatessen nearby. When I returned, Lavinia was at the door to meet me.

"Thanks very much, dear," she said as I handed her the grocery bag. "Now, you go home now."

"It's been very nice."

"Yes, it *has*," she said.

"I'll telephone you soon, all right?"

"That would be nice. Goodbye." She smiled. Her eyes, even squinted against the outdoors, were bright and alive.

I walked home, excited and enthusiastic, as if I'd just had a first date. And I suppose, in a way, I had.

Lavinia. Lavinia! Of course, I telephoned Lavinia. We arranged that I would visit her the next week. She was cordial, but not effusive, on the phone. Those seven days went by slowly, I have to say. I was—well, I suppose I was smitten. I guess I had a kind of crush on Lavinia, and like a teenager with a crush, I was full of heightened uncertainties. I was secretly worried that the second visit wouldn't be as delightful as the first. And then I had a million questions, all of them eventually leading to one big one: who was Lavinia?

I stepped into her apartment, then, the next time, feeling a disturbing mixture of anticipation and skepticism. I was hopeful, but guarded. I greeted her a little too warmly. She seemed genuinely pleased to have me there again. She was dressed in what I would come to see as her basic Lavinia outfit, an old shapeless housedress and slippers. It was evident after a short while that she had totally forgotten my name. She had a cigarette in her hand. She usually did, I was to find. The entire apartment had that ubiquitous odor of deeply penetrated smoke many apartments had in those days. It rose from the furniture, it came at you from the bathroom towels, it even seemed to linger inside the refrigerator. It's a smell I suspect that is largely unfamiliar to the most recent, largely non-smoking generation.

"I've always wondered," she began talking even before she reached her chair, "what men *do* with prostitutes."

I was taken aback. I think I might have even stammered.

"I mean," she went on, "after they do their business, do they *talk*, or what?" She was seated now. She waved her cigarette around in a flourish.

"Well..." I began, not at all certain how much detail I should provide. I wasn't sure Lavinia really wanted firsthand knowledge.

"I used to ask Alec, and he would say, 'Damn it, *I don't know* what they do, because I've never been to one!'"

That name again. Alec.

"I don't think you do much chatting," I said.

"I was always terribly naïve about those kinds of things," she said. "I remember going up to Harlem one time. That was *years* ago." She tried to moisten her lips, which were almost always dry, with a quick flick of her tongue. The feeble light from her window highlighted her russet hair. She continued:

"I think I was nineteen. I don't know how I got away from Mother, but I must have. A *shoe* salesman asked me out for a date." When she spoke the word *shoe,* her voice seemed to drop two or three octaves. "After dinner we went up to his room. For a drink, I suppose. I certainly didn't think anything was going to happen.

"All I remember about his room was that he had rows and rows and rows of shoes lined up against the wall. All sorts and sizes. *Hun*dreds of shoes." She paused and plucked a tiny piece of tobacco from her lips. "Well, I didn't know anything about sex. Com*plete*ly ignorant. And at one point—I guess he had given me my drink by then—he started to take off his clothes."

"He did?"

"Yes."

"What did you do?"

"I just started to *cry*." She laughed. She laughed at her own youthful clumsiness. The story wasn't finished, though. She took a quick puff of her cigarette and went on. "Well, the man started to get upset. 'Don't cry!' he said. 'For God's sake, *don't cry*!' He gave me ten dollars to take a cab home. So, I left. I rang for the elevator, and when it came, the bellboy was inside. I must have still had the ten dollars sticking out of my hand, because the bellboy looked at me, and at the money, and said, 'You probably could've gotten more than that, honey.'"

I roared. Lavinia leaned slowly back in her chair. "And Alec said to me, 'You couldn't have been *that* ignorant.' But I was!"

"Who's Alec, if you don't mind me asking?"

"Oh, Alec. Alec was my *greatest* friend. Alec Wilder. I don't suppose you've heard of him.

"No, sorry, I haven't."

Something nagged at me, though. Somewhere, I did know the name.

"Was he famous?"

Lavinia threw her head back. "Oh, Lord, no. Celebrated, you might say. No, dear, he was a composer. Did you ever hear of a song called 'I'll Be Around'?"

"No."

"Well, it's a haunting song. Exquisitely beautiful. You should listen to it. Alec composed it."

And then it hit me. When I was a student at the University of Michigan, I would listen occasionally to a program on National Public Radio about American music, and Alec Wilder had been the host. I liked the program very much, and the main reason I did was because of Wilder. He was smart, informed, witty, and engaging. I didn't know a thing about him, and I don't think I'd thought about him since. But I remembered thoroughly enjoying the program. And I remembered that his qualities pierced even a self-absorbed college student's indifference.

I told Lavinia about that. And then she told me the story of their friendship. Not all of it, because it was a long one, full of great moments, with highs and lows, that lasted over twenty years. Alec Wilder was a staunch individualist, lived only in hotels, never married, had inherited money, did not suffer fools, was friends with Sinatra and other well-known musicians—Mabel Mercer was his favorite—and had a razor wit. Lavinia worshiped him. ("We never *did* anything, you understand.") Wilder was to be a third person during my visits with Lavinia, a specter, always ready, through his medium, Lavinia, to add a comment or to make an elaboration. Lavinia spoke of him with as much conviction as if he were sitting next to her, or to me. Lavinia's two marriages had failed, but not this friendship. It had been the beacon of her life. I was to get to know Alec Wilder well in the next two years, and I can tell you that he was a compelling man, *is* a compelling man. If you want to get an idea of his acerbic wit, have a look at his book, *Letters I Never Mailed*. It's wonderful stuff. Three are to Lavinia.

Oh, if I wasn't in love, I was tottering on the edge of falling.

I think now as I look back on it all, I realize that part of the reason for my infatuation was this: If Lavinia, at eighty-one, could be this droll, this acerbic, this sharp, this verbally agile and entertaining, well, then, maybe when *I* was eighty-one, I might be, too. Maybe old age could actually be not just dignified, but graceful.

I don't remember too much about the rest of that visit. Lavinia talked a bit about the woman who cleaned her apartment. "A darling girl," she said, "but she's very fat and has the foulest mouth I've ever heard." I left her after about an hour. I made sure we have a definite appointment for my next visit.

My visits to Lavinia eased into a kind of routine. I was working as a freelance advertising copywriter at the time. Since my job—feast or famine it was—could often provide me with considerable windows of free time, I was usually able to arrange to see Lavinia during the week, and during the day. She seemed to prefer that I come in the afternoon, and that was fine with me. I was always glad to see her, and I think she was glad to see me. She would sit down heavily behind her note-cluttered desk, and I would pull up a chair next to her. (I had advanced from the distant couch.) Even before I settled in, she would reach for a cigarette, light it, and begin talking.

As the weeks went by, I learned more about her. She had been married twice, and both husbands were dead. She had three children, two girls and a boy, all grown. The youngest girl was married and had recently adopted a baby from South America. The oldest girl was gay. The boy was married, lived in California, and was a writer. He supported his writing by doing odd jobs. For years, Lavinia had worked in Scribner's bookstore in New York City. This was how she had made her living after her divorces and after her husbands had died.

For those of you who never saw that bookstore, Scribner's—and never will, since it's gone forever—I want say a word about it. I went there many times. It was regal. It disappeared about ten years ago, became a sweater store and now is something else. It was located on Fifth Avenue around 49th Street, in that same magical parameter that includes Saks Fifth Avenue, St. Patrick's Cathedral and Rockefeller Center. It was a wonderful bookstore, of the old kind, with a second tier made of dark wrought iron that wound around the inside, like a widow's walk. The bookstore was a shrine to writers, because Scribner's was the house that had published Fitzgerald, Hemingway, Lardner, and Wolfe. Scribner's was Maxwell Perkins' house. You felt enriched browsing there.

For the past twenty years, ever since the second husband died, Lavinia had lived alone. Alone, but not uncontent, I suspect. I think probably she was better suited to being by herself. Her apartment, as I said, was small and simply furnished and dark. On one wall of her living room hung a Renoir reproduction, her sole effort at bringing color to her surroundings. She wasn't much of a decorator. Lined up against the wall opposite her desk were rows and rows of books, mostly hardbacks from the 1940s and 50s. There was a smattering of recent titles, too. Her favorite author was John Galsworthy, a writer I didn't know well at all. Lavinia was a proud, card-carrying anglophile. Books were crucial to her, and she treated them as old, valued friends. Occasionally, she loaned me a book, and if I didn't return it by, say, three weeks, she would drop a heavy hint like, "Now, dear, there's no *hurry,* but that book, you know...."

Somewhere in the middle of all these books was a black wall phone. A small niche had been made for it that would often be closed up by the tottering books. Next to it, Lavinia had stationed a big rocking chair. It was here, after haltingly walking over to quiet the phone's brutal, insistent ring and addressing it angrily as she did with an "Oh, shut *up!*" that she would sit back and take her calls. She didn't mind talking on the phone, but she hated dialing a number. Her eyes and fingers weren't up to it. Periodically, I would be called upon to do it for her.

I soon came to know that what Lavinia revealed about herself she did in a masterfully haphazard manner. Names were thrown out as if I should already have known them. The past and present were often mixed together wonderfully, like a big, complicated chef's salad. Characters dead and alive were spoken of in the same breath without so much a nod as to that one critical difference between them. Perhaps in Lavinia's mind there wasn't a difference. What I came to know came to me completely without warning. This was how I found out she had a son. I had known she had two daughters, but the third child had evaded me. It was if the son had been hiding behind the couch and one day just popped up and said hello. I discovered her second husband in the same manner, hiding behind that couch.

This lack of adherence to traditional narrative form gave the relationship, at least from my viewpoint, a fanciful, improvisational-like quality. I liked that. Right up until our last visit, I felt Lavinia might surprise me with some major fact of her life—that, for example, someone else lived with her in the apartment (which wasn't the case)—blithely tossing out the information as if it were nothing.

What did we talk about those first heady months? Off the top of my head I remember discussing politics, books, the Kennedys (she despised Joseph Kennedy, Sr.), that famed Scribner's bookstore where she had worked for so long, movie stars (She loved Jack Nicholson: "I'm *mad* about him."), her childhood in Buffalo, New York, her neighbors, television ("You'll never hear me say a bad word about it. It keeps old people like me from being too lonely."), money ("I'd love a *boat*ful."), birds ("Can't *stand* them. Those horrible dirty little *feet*!"), and a crazy quilt of other things, from the ridiculous to the sublime—including growing old and dying.

These were two subjects that I was eager to talk about but which, in a thousand years, I wouldn't have dared to introduce. It was Lavinia who brought them up herself. She brought them up calmly and evenly as if she were talking about a shopping list. Lavinia had a perfectly uncomplicated view of growing old. She loathed it with every fiber in her body. She was only too aware of every malfunction, every decay of her physical being, and she was resentful.

"If there is a God," she said when one of her arthritic knees was particularly disturbing her, rubbing it petulantly, "when I see Him the first thing I'm going to ask Him is, '*Why* do we have to grow *old*? Why can't we be like one of those big wonderful trees in the forest that simply..." And here she made a long, slow swooping movement with her hand, "...fall down when it's time? That would be so much more *dignified.*" She looked straight at me, her cloudy eyes narrowing with anger and frustration.

In those moments I would feel a deep, deep inadequacy. What could I do? Oh, I wanted to heal her, to make her young again! Or at least to arrest the process, the descent. I'm also ashamed to say that this rawness fascinated me. I was being admitted into an extremely private room, one that represented the final stage of a journey we only take once. Intimacy on that level—if level is the word—is exciting, whether we like to admit it or not. It was at a price, though. The melancholic attacks brought on by her body could put her into a dark cave of a mood from which she often wouldn't emerge for days. Often we would sit and stare at each other for minutes at a time.

About death itself, Lavinia was of two minds. On the one hand, she could show a sense of outright dread. She could also speak about her own death with an almost child-like curiosity: "I can't *wait* to find out," she would say. "I'm wild to know what's *there.*" Did I believe her? Yes, I did. She was so convincing, I almost wanted to go with her.

After about eight or nine visits, I felt comfortable enough to go beyond what had become my accustomed role as the listener. I realized that if this were going to develop into a genuine friendship, it, like all genuine friendships, would have to be balanced. And I *wanted* us to be friends. It wasn't that Lavinia discouraged me from talking. Not at all. It was just that in the face of such an utterly fresh personality I chose to stand back and be all ears. One day, that changed. I guess I no longer considered my visits to Lavinia to be some sort of charity work—if, indeed, they ever were.

I was glad I began talking. Lavinia turned out to be an equally marvelous listener. She was attentive, even rapt at times, and she was just as enthusiastic and forthright with her comments and counsel as she was about everything else. Even if her responses were not in the form of maxims or proverbs but merely commands—"Don't *wor*ry about that!"—her pure commitment to them made them seem irrefutable. It wasn't long before I was telling her the story of my life.

I told her how for years I'd wanted to quit advertising and be a *real* writer.

"Well, why haven't you, dear?" she asked.

"I guess I'm afraid," I said. I hated admitting that. I was being honest, at least.

"Go *do* it," she said. "Don't even think twice."

"What if...."

She waved her cigarette about dismissively.

"Don't *think* too much about it, dear. That's your downfall." She puffed her cigarette. "Go *write*. Now."

And she was right. I *did* think too much about these things.

"You know," she said after a small pause, "*I've* written some books."

"You?"

Lavinia huffed herself up in righteous indignation—and well she should have.

"Oh," I said fumbling, "I didn't mean...I mean...."

"I have," she said, with dramatized dignity, "written four or five."

What an idiot I was. I tried desperately to recover.

"Really? What are they?"

"Well, my *fav*orite is one I wrote for children. It's called *Over the Hills and Far Away*."

"Do you have a copy?"

She pointed to her overstocked bookcase. "Somewhere in all that confusion."

"I'd love to see it."

Lavinia got up slowly and walked with difficulty to the bookcase.

"Come here, dear, will you."

I joined her. She squinted at the spines of the books. "It's here somewhere," she said, sweeping her hand across a row near the bottom. "See if you can find it."

In a minute, I did. "Yes, here it is." I plucked out the book. Indeed, she had written a young adult novel, as they're called now. "May I take it home and read it?"

"If you swear by all that's holy that you'll return it."

"Yes, I do. I will."

Lavinia, it turned out, had written four books—*published* four books—and had been the editor of a fifth. And how many books had I written? None! Later, I tracked them all down. I was most delighted by—and still am—her book called *A High Old Time: Or How to Enjoy Being a Woman Over Sixty*. It's a splendidly written book, full of sharply spiced aphorisms, and it has *personality*. It falls easily into that category of books written by high-spirited, witty, literate women who have a no-nonsense approach to life.

Lavinia loved good manners, and wit, and humor and decency. And character. It's all there in her book. This, of course, is what distinguishes people ultimately, isn't it? What they do, and how they do it. It takes some of us a long time to understand this, because we are susceptible to glitter and rhetorical flourishes and all sorts of personality con artists who enter our lives. When these people disappear, we wonder what happened, and we're left questioning our own judgment—or, more to the point, our own needs. So, sitting in that small room with Lavinia, who was dressed in her drab housedress and worn slippers, I was smart enough to know how lucky I was to be with the genuine article.

Lavinia was repelled by bad manners and vulgarity as much as she was attracted to grace and to wit and to honesty. Her rants were as enjoyable to listen to as were her commendations. More so. These things *mattered* to Lavinia. She despised self-pity, for example. That word *despise* is so apt. When she didn't like something, she didn't like it with her full body—from her narrowed, fixed eyes down to her tensed knees and arched toes. It was wonderfully entertaining to be in the presence of such an able despiser, especially when her subjects were people or traits that deserve to be despised.

And so self-pity was at the top of her list of behavior to be banned forever. Here's what she says about it in *A High Old Time*:

> Anecdotes rooted in self-pity are excruciating bores, for self-pity is a bore. Its only fascinating aspect is that if you feel sorry for yourself, nobody else feels under any obligation to feel sorry for you. You're doing too successful a job of it yourself to invite their compassion. Have you ever by mistake put in a dress whose colors bleed with white clothes in a washing machine? Everything else in the machine is ruined,

because the dye spreads so virulently. And so it is with self-pity: it can discolor anything you do or say.

So it was humiliating for her, I know, when the tyranny of old age began to wear her down, and she would complain.

Spurred on by Lavinia, I began to make plans. Plans that would eventually take me out of advertising forever and, for a year, out of the country.

Meanwhile, the visits continued. So many wonderful moments there were. Lavinia told me the story of her marriages, both of which were bad. Her second husband she particularly didn't like. He used to belittle her. They had nothing in common. I asked her why she'd married him in the first place, and she said, "I don't remember." They were living in a house somewhere, and one night he had to go downstairs to the basement to fix something. And she said,

"So he opened the door to the basement, and just as he was standing there at the top of the stairs I…."

Lavinia raised both her hands, palms outward.

"You mean," I said, "you were going to push him down the stairs?"

She nodded slightly. "I thought it would look like an accident."

I laughed. It was *funny*.

"But you didn't."

"No. Didn't have the courage." She took a puff of her cigarette.

"But you came close."

She smiled. "Just wanted to….*umph*!" And here she actually did make a good, strong pushing motion, finally getting the satisfaction, vicarious as it was, she'd deprived herself of years ago. I looked with glee as I imagined the boor tumbling down the stairs, getting what he deserved.

Now, you tell me, how could you not fall in love with a woman like that?

In all the time I knew her, I think we went outside three times. Because of her arthritic knees, walking for her was arduous, but her doctor told her she must walk, and so once in a while, complaining about his tyranny, she asked me if I would walk with her. We didn't walk far, just over to Fifth Avenue and down to Washington Square Park where we would sit for a while before returning to her apartment. Lavinia held onto my arm as we walked, and didn't say anything. I think she might have been in pain, or perhaps she was simply concentrating so as not to stumble. Her pace was determinately slow. She wasn't particularly happy about being outdoors, but it always made me feel better to know that I had gotten her out for a bit. She looked so pale in the sunlight, like a cloistered nun.

One day—this is now deep into our relationship—I arrived ready to take Lavinia out for one of those infrequent walks. We'd planned it on the phone. I found her glum and terse. When I asked her what was wrong, she wouldn't answer me. She wouldn't even smoke a cigarette. She just sat there, mute. It took me quite a while to get her to come forth, and even then I could only extract words bit by bit. Finally, in a great effort, and full of self-recrimination, she said,

"I'm dep*res*sed!" She barely looked at me.

I didn't know what to say. Not that Lavinia couldn't be down. She could be upset about the pain in her legs and about her penchant for forgetting things. She would rant about those plagues eloquently. I'd never heard her use the word "depressed" about herself, though. It wouldn't have been in character.

"But why?" I asked, and quickly groped for a reason. "Is it your legs?"

"No, honey. No." She spoke with the slightest condescension, as if something so trivial could hardly be the cause.

"Your eyes?"

She shook her head slowly. Then, her lips trembling, with great difficulty she forced herself to speak,

"I'm just afraid I'll...end up in one of those...*homes*."

I'm not doing justice to the great fear that pervaded her confession. Her eyes were stark raving full of it. It was naked helplessness. When she finished telling me this, she looked up at me, her mouth twitching. Her eyes began to water. She was totally afraid.

"But…but why do you think you'll be sent to a home?" I asked.

"I don't know. I'm just getting…. Nothing *works* any more." She stole a quick, humiliated glance at me.

"Well, a few things may be on he blink," I said, trying to sound authentic, "but you won't be going to any home."

She forced a half smile on her face.

If I were being honest, though, I knew she had grounds. Who was to say that some day she might decline so profoundly she wouldn't be able to walk from her bedroom to her bathroom? Who was to say those cursed legs of hers might not give out altogether? Who was to say that old age, relentless and unsparing as the wind, might not come to her one too many times? Who was to say she might not have to go to a home?

I tried my best to cajole her out of this black mood. She looked at me, dubious and still trembling. I think she may have reached out a hand to me, but I can't be sure. My mind is clouded by the intensity. I do know I felt closer to Lavinia than I ever had. She was in a pitiable state: She was completely helpless.

By the time I left that day, Lavinia seemed to be feeling better. I was still worried, though. I called her that evening to check on how she was. She thanked me for my help and said she was fine now, dear, thank you. She attempted to minimize how bad she had felt. "Oh, it was one of those *moods* I get in, that's all. They always pass. I'm *mor*tified that I complained." But this seemed to me to signal a change. Lavinia was growing old in the way she loathed and feared.

In the meantime, I had been following her advice. I had resolved to quit advertising and to do what I always had wanted to do. *Write.* I had stashed away as much money as I could in my bank account from my freelance work. Those were the days when you could make a bundle as a freelance advertising copywriter. Money and work were everywhere. I managed to get a job for six months that paid extremely well. My goal was to save enough money to go to the South of France for a year. And to write. It was now or never, I thought. Lavinia had helped put me over the edge by giving me a verbal shove now and then. I knew this was what I wanted, and needed. I had already made a deposit on a house to rent in a remote village in Provence. It was owned by an American couple, and it was cheap. I figured I had about two month's more work, and I'd be ready to go. I'd have enough money to live on for a year over there.

I told Lavinia about my plan one day. I thought she'd be thrilled for me.

"Oh, really, dear?" she said, when I told her about my plans to leave New York.

"Yes, and *you* are partially responsible for my being able to do it."

"Me? I had nothing to do with it. It's *you* who did it."

I didn't sense the pride and enthusiasm I was expecting from my decision.

"So, what do you think?" I was eager to be seen as her protégé.

"Think? I think it's wonderful, if that's what you want to do."

Her tone was somewhat flat. She of course knew this is what I wanted to do.

I left that day irritated with her. I didn't think I wanted much. Just a slap on the back, maybe, or a *good for you*.

I stayed away for two weeks. It was out of spite, and that was out of being hurt by Lavinia's response to my life-changing plans. I guess you could say I was trying to punish her. I'm not especially proud to admit this, but I'm not especially ashamed, either. But of course I was *leaving* her. And why should she celebrate that? I knew she was happy that I seemed to have found the courage to do what I wanted to do, but that wasn't the point, was it? I was cutting off something. I wasn't going to be visiting her anymore. She had reached out to me, and now I was pushing her away.

Then something struck deep into me. A shock of self-recognition. *What if,* I thought, *what if* I get over there and nothing happens? What if I can't do this without Lavinia there with me? And then in a fantastical shift of interpretation, I began to see Lavinia as leaving *me.* How could she do this?

Then one day toward the time I was supposed to leave for France, I came to visit. I walked into the familiar living room and saw Lavinia seated behind her desk, customary cigarette in her hand, big glass ashtray in front of her. I strolled toward her desk breezily. I stopped short. I saw something out of the corner of my eye. I turned. There, seated on the couch, was a young woman. I have the recollection my jaw dropped. In my bewilderment I was still able to see that the young woman was very pretty and, most memorably, had a wide, open smile and vivid eyes. I think I may have even stammered. I felt like Goldilocks. I was probably an inch away from saying, "But who's that sitting on my couch?"

"Hello, dear," Lavinia said. "I want you to meet...Bobby."

Bobby smiled and waved at me.

"Dear," Lavinia said to Bobby, "this is..." her voice trailed off. She scowled and closed her eyes. "This is..."

"Richard," I said.

"Of *course* it's Richard," Lavinia said.

"Hello," I said to Bobby. And she said it back to me.

I didn't stay long. I walked outside. *What right did I have to be jealous?* I asked myself. But I was. I felt like Iago. After that day, I think I made one more visit to Lavinia. The plans for my trip were beginning to take over everything else. I did want to say goodbye, though. I did want to tell her how much these last two years had meant to me. And they had meant so much to me. They had.

And so I left. I went to Provence. I lived in Provence for a year, a marvelous time. I wrote Lavinia letters, sporadically, and sent her postcards. I got no replies from her, but that didn't concern me. She could only write with great difficulty, and her script was nearly impenetrable. Toward the middle of the year, my letters began to taper off, and then the cards, and then I stopped writing her altogether. So much was going on in France that was changing me, making me grow and flourish, and so much of it was thrilling and all encompassing. I didn't have much room for Lavinia.

And then the year was over.

When I came home, I did think of Lavinia once again. What was she doing? How was she? A few weeks after I had resettled myself in my apartment, I called her. A woman—not Lavinia—answered the phone. I asked to speak with Lavinia.

"Who is this, please?"

Right away, I knew. We always do. The news is in the tone, even if the words are hintlessly ordinary. I knew Lavinia was dead. I knew she was dead, and that I would never see her again.

I told the woman on the phone who I was, and explained how I knew Lavinia. It was Lavinia's daughter. I hadn't recognized her voice.

"Lavinia died," she said. "She died about two weeks ago."

"*Oh, no.*"

"Yes, it's very sad."

I don't care how many times we go through it, it's still a cold stark shock to hear the words. *Dead.* No more. Does not exist. How can you fathom that?

I spoke with Lavinia's daughter for a few minutes. I was curious about her death. "Was it an easy death?"

"No. It was horrible. The last few months were just horrible."

I shook my head, as if she could see me. I didn't want her to elaborate. I could imagine, though. I gave her my condolences, and told her how much Lavinia had given me, and how much I admired her, and always would, and then I hung up.

So, she didn't get her wish after all. She didn't die like one of those big wonderful trees in the forest that simply fall down. The injustice of it! Well, she knew the whole thing was unjust, this growing old. She knew that. Still.

Then I thought about her vision of that wonderful old tree just falling to earth. I thought how rare and unlikely that really is. When an old tree falls in the woods, it's usually stopped from completing its descent by other, more robust trees adjacent to it. Sometimes when I come upon a tree that's caught like that, I have the notion to go over and push it down, to free it from the restraining tree so it can fall down and die. I'm always surprised at how difficult it is to push the dead tree free. Even if I push hard, applying all my body weight, it resists. I walk away frustrated, and, strangely, feeling as if the tree were somehow ungrateful.

Ridiculous, isn't it, to think like that? It isn't I who am to determine when the tree will fall to the earth. It isn't the tree itself, either. It's something else. Lavinia had to live and die with it. I will, too.

Surrendering to Provence

It was a stone house that was big and old with many rooms and walls as thick as a fortress. We lived there for a year in a small village in a corner of Provence about an hour from Avignon. My Dutch girlfriend and I were escaping New York City—just had had enough. Where would we go? To the South of France. And why not? We had the fortune to find this place outside of time. It was a lovely way to live, in a house that had been built 200 years ago, hewn out of stone found not in quarries but in the fields. It wasn't easy at first, though. The village life seemed as durable and unchanging as the house, and as mute. It was a while before the woman I loved and I could begin to fathom the rhythm of its ways. Why didn't the villagers respond to our greetings, except for the briefest answers? Why weren't they the least bit interested in us? Why didn't they accept us with open arms?

A village in Provence can be exquisite and maddening. It took time for us to see that our sojourn was merely a blink in the villagers' unwavering eyes. We did, at last, and it was the land that led us. As she and I woke up day after day to a sun-flooded room, our casement windows open to the new morning, we began to become part of Provence. We couldn't look out onto the softly undulating hills, with their legions of precisely lined vine plants, without giving away our hearts. We couldn't smell the subtle morning air, a perfume of everything that grew there, without becoming a little more lost in love. We couldn't have our vision enhanced by the marvel of the light without wanting never to leave.

The gap between their ways and ours lessened, and that was in part due to the power of the place. We were under its sway, and so many of the things that were important to the villagers became important to us. We walked the rough little hills above the village and saw wild thyme growing. The plant is like a dwarf version of a stunted tundra tree, all twisted and leaning. It's a tough thing, difficult to cut. I began using it in my cooking. I soon found the taste is not the same as domesticated thyme. Like many wild versions of a plant or spice we know, its flavor is more subtle and quieter, and more interesting. It's a good metaphor for some of the villagers we met. They were wild thyme. Their tastes weren't revealed just by a single encounter.

No, we'd never be *paysans*—as the villagers unhesitatingly called themselves. Not farmers, peasants. They were people rooted to the land. Eventually, most everything in Provence comes back to the land. It is as basic and rooted as the thyme that grew above the village. *Pays*, the root word of *paysan,* means "country." Before you leave Provence, walk in the *maquis* or the *garrigue*, the scrub hills, full of dry wonders and simplicity. Let yourself become part of this remarkable land. Day by day, we surrendered to its spirit.

In surrender, Provence simplified our lives. That's what the place will do. Simplicity will come over anyone who stays there for even more than a few days. "Only in this sun-steeped country," Colette writes, "can a heavy table, a wicker chair, an earthenware jar crowned with flowers, and a dish whose thick enameling has run over the edge, make a complete furnishing." And we began to understand, like everyone else who has become attached to Provence, that there is no place on earth like it. No one can possibly prepare you for this consistently ethereal level of beauty. Not any book, movie, or essay. Not these words. No painting. Nowhere else do you find such a confluence of pellucid air, fierce sun, ravishing smells and tastes, and grace.

It may not be your country, but it is not altogether foreign to you, either. As M.F.K. Fisher said of her first visit to Aix-en-Provence, "I was once more in my own place, an invader of what was already mine." It may be singular, but you can become its citizen. You may feel as if you were born there, and perhaps you were.

We had a used car we had bought, scruffy and prone to seizures, but on the whole reliable. In it, we ventured near and far in the South of France and came to see much more of the land beyond our village during that year. We went to nearby Avignon first. What a shock it was to go from our little hamlet, with its stubbornly self-important ways, to a city that has had such a prominent role on the world stage! We—at least I—felt Avignon is a sad place. Even though it's on the lyrical Rhône, that magnificent water, the city has a melancholy air. Cities have lived lives, too, and when you walk them, you begin to see exactly who they have become. I think of Avignon as not at peace with itself. For that very reason, it's impossible to forget.

We drove to Aix, that exquisite town, then on to palm-lined Nice and to Menton. We went to the Gorges du Verdon in Haute Provence, Colorado in France, except that Colorado is far too young to have the ancient sense those small, high villages possess. Haute Provence, walking realm of Provence's greatest writer, Jean Giono, whose rare, dignified sensibility reflects the land and the people he loved. We drove to Apt and to old Gordes, and wound our way to its top as so many others have, rapt. We drove to Arles and to les Baux and to the Camargue, and to the moving village of Aigues Mortes, and to the gypsy enclave at St.-Marie.

We went to St.-Rémy in search of van Gogh's ghost, and then walked the sun-scorched hills nearby, the Alpilles, which he painted. We drove to Marseilles, a city as unjustly feared as New York, and that's a pity, because Marseilles is so sharply flavored and so alive. M.F.K. Fisher described the Marseilles she loved as "mysterious, unknowable," and it will haunt you and draw you back as it did her. We went to Nîmes and walked into its amphitheater and felt dread and awe at the Roman Empire. We drove to L'Isle-sur-la-Sorgue and watched trout swimming in the cool little stream and stayed in that pretty place until dusk at a table outdoors. We saw all these wonders and many more, and we continued to make forays into the heart of the heart of Provence all year.

But no matter how far we went, we always came home to our village. To the well-wrought house that now was our home. To the simplicity and timelessness of a life that unfolded before us. We met everyone in the place, and we began to piece together their lives. We were even luckier to find work in the fields, so we experienced Provence's light and air and scents throughout the long days. The wine tasted better in our dirt-caked hands, and so did the *daube* I cooked for us when the day was through. They paid us, too, in francs, by God!

It was a privilege to go to sleep weary in our village, and to wake up with that slight feeling of regret physical labor bestows on you every morning. We had the gift of responsibility in Provence, and how much luckier can two people get? You cannot steal idle moments when everything is given to you. We were not used to the hard work, to the bending, pulling, digging and planting. We were old people for an hour every morning, but nothing in the world would have induced us to quit. We went home to lunch midday as the villagers did. We spooned our soup and devoured our bread happily with the morning's cool still hovering over us. Sundays became as precious to us as long-waited vacations. Nothing that year was sweeter than buying villagers we liked a *pastis* with money we earned working their land. If you can work in Provence, even for a single day, you should do it.

Despite the fact that we were frugal and that we worked, we could see our money dwindling. This alarmed us, and saddened us. We didn't want to leave. We wanted to stay forever. We had brought a dog with us to Provence, and in our desperation to stay longer, we hatched a plan. We decided to teach her to hunt for truffles. Dogs as well as pigs hunt for truffles in Provence, and if we could turn our Brooklyn-born stray into a truffle-finder, we'd be flush. We heard that a man had a dog in a village not far from us who could find truffles, but we never found him. We bought a jar of cheap truffles in our local supermarket—perhaps they were from Bulgaria—and made her sniff these oily black things six or seven times a day for a week. Then one day we drove her to the woods where the villagers said if there were truffles, they had to be there. We whispered in our dog's ear, "Go find truffles! Find truffles!" and let her go. She ran about, delighted. She paused at a spot near the foot of a small oak tree. Hadn't she? Perfect! We brought our shovels and began to dig.

Five holes later, truffleless, and drenched in sweat, we drove home.

So, we had to leave. We had to return to New York City, to that city we no longer felt was our home and wondered if it could ever be again. (It could.) We had to say goodbye to Provence, and to the village we had grown to love and that had taken root in our souls. We all have to say goodbye to Provence sooner or later, and when we come home we all spend the next months or years dreaming of the place. We dote on our memories like political exiles that long to return to the mother country. We'll talk to anyone who will listen to us about its marvels. Sooner or later, we'll come back, we know. It's just a matter of when. It might be ten years, or twelve, but we'll come back. So far, Provence is stronger than anything we have brought to it, or done to it. Pray that never changes.

Colette's words I quoted are from her book, *Break of Day*. If you love Provence, or you are going to Provence for the first time, you must read it. The prose is as potent and sensual as those Dionysian scents distilled from Provençal flowers in Grasse. Colette had a house in St.-Tropez, and she began staying there before that fishing village was anointed by Parisians to become famous. *Break of Day* was published in 1928, but not an observation is obsolete. Her house was above the village, and she writes about gardening, the movements of the day, her animals, and the people who come and go, and the delicious sensual tastes of the place. Here, Mother Nature doesn't wear a silky dress, she walks naked. Colette writes with a pen dipped in sun, oil, sweat, and salt.

"What a country!" she exclaims. "The invader endows it with villas and garages, with motorcars and dance-halls built to look like *Mas*. But during the course of the centuries how many ravishers have not fallen in love with such a captive? They arrive plotting to ruin her, stop suddenly and listen to her breathing in her sleep, and then, turning silent and respectful, they softly shut the gate in the fence. Submissive to your wishes, Provence…they have no other desire, Beauty, than to serve you and enjoy it."

Go. Submit. Surrender.

Maine Journal

My former wife and I began spending summer weeks on a small island off the coast of Maine when our daughter was just two years old. It was our annual great escape from New York City. We rented the same house each year—a large, old, wide-porched glory that faces out to the sea. The island had many lessons to teach all of us, and they have been rich and unforgettable. Since we began coming to the island, my wife and I have divorced. The island remains steadfastly there for our daughter, though, and she continues to spend part of her summer there each year with her mother. While I was there, I kept a journal. These are a few of the entries, expanded later.

Sweetwater Island, August 17

This small island off Maine's southern coast is made almost entirely of solid rock. The vegetation has a sense of victory about it, having defied the granite ground, and established its green and woody self here in myriad forms. Sweetwater Island (a pseudonym, as are the names of all the people) is an island of just forty houses. It has no shops, only one truck, sells no gas on its dock and did not have town water until last year. It relied on the spring water for which it is named.

It does have a post office. It may be the smallest in Maine. It's certainly not the least busy. The postmaster, John Weston, sells thousands of dollars of stamps every year. This island, with a total of forty-seven acres, could not have more than two hundred people at one time, and the total number of people who visit during the summer probably does not exceed four hundred. Yet, such is John Weston's sense of mission, that day visitors and renters find themselves mailing in requests for stamps during the winter months from New York, Denver, Orlando, Los Angeles.

But Sweetwater Island is that kind of place. It inspires transcontinental loyalties. It is a beautiful place with a large, eclectic palette of weather. At one moment you might be watching a brilliant sun illuminating the water, while—literally—the next, that water will be shrouded in a mysterious cotton, a slow moving, deathly quiet fog. There are rocky shores and tides that wane and wax in huge strides, leaving yards and yards of sea bottom exposed twice a day only to be swallowed whole twice a day again.

The wildlife is foreign to anyone who resides south of New Hampshire. There are seal, their sleek dark heads bobbing up from the deep a few feet away from your boat; they take quick, furtive account, and disappear. There are ospreys, those noble fishers and loyal parents, with their haughty, Medici profiles. Their high-pitched shrieks regularly mark the day. There are cormorants, bobbing about and, suddenly, plunging headfirst below. There are loons occasionally, and eagles, too. And a solitary, stately blue heron.

The ocean water that envelopes Sweetwater Island is of a clarity that will confound anyone who has spent most of their ocean time in, say, North Carolina or California. The seawater is pure, and clear, and has an almost Bahamian quality to it, except for the electric cold. It is still salt water, though, and so the experience of wading in it—few can tolerate its low temperature for a swim—has the best of the salt- and fresh-water worlds: buoyancy and lucidity.

With all this wildness, the island is surprisingly benign. There are no snakes, no raccoons (except rare, wayward families that are quickly deported), no deer, no skunks, no moose, and no bear. There is just the barest minimum of poison ivy, and it's a trial to find it. There are mosquitoes, no denying that. It wouldn't be Maine without them. They are certainly not welcome, and they raise wide welts on children's legs, but pitted against all its virtues, the island can tolerate them, and does.

Sweetwater Island, August 18

Families began coming to Sweetwater Island in the last years of the nineteenth century. They came from Portland, Boston, and even as far away as Baltimore. (Today, they come from Denver and Los Angeles.) They would take steamboats up from the big cities and be dropped off on this Maine island to spend June, July and August in the thralls of serenity. You can see an old steamboat schedule tacked on the side of the boathouse on Sweetwater's sole dock. Part of the ethos of those who summer here is a determined effort to keep Sweetwater Island pretty much the way it was when their grandparents or great-grandparents first summered here. A surprisingly big hotel was constructed here in the early part of the 20th century, the Algonquin, and you could sleep and eat there, and drink the fabled delicious cold island spring water and completely forget the metropolis you left behind.

Soon, some of the families who made annual pilgrimages to Sweetwater Island foresaw that the Algonquin might not be there waiting for them forever, and so they banded together and bought the island. They built the houses that, with only few new additions (the last was in the 1960s), remain here still. The grandchildren of those pioneers can remember eating breakfast at the Algonquin, and then seeing it close, and, ultimately, crumble. There is, save for the occasional crockery shard someone finds, nothing left of the establishment that drew visitors from as far away as Chicago. (There are black and white photographs of the hotel in the island's little museum, for new visitors.) But the houses are still here, and the descendants who reside in them are just as devoted to their island as their pioneering ancestors were. With their chauvinism about the island that can sometimes appear xenophobic, they are probably not unhappy at the hotel's demise.

While other communities may have had a similar goal to preserve their summer Edens in their original states, Sweetwater Island has largely succeeded. The islanders have done this, and continue to do so, with a hawk-eyed vigilance for maintaining what they see as the island's character—really, its soul. And by an almost paranoiac silence about its very existence. (If the islanders knew

I was writing about their island, even in disguise, they would be horrified.)

Indeed, if some of the first residents from Boston or Portland were to somehow show up today, they would not find themselves out of place. These archetypical nineteenth-century visitors would have plenty in common with their twenty-first-century fellow islanders. They could jump into the latest conversation about dock improvements, boardwalk repairs, and the vole problem with fluent ease.

What residents of Sweetwater Island want—and what they work hard to realize—is a place where a child can feel summer as his or her parents did: with great, almost unrestricted zeal. A place where a child can *become* the summer and where he or she and nature can forge singular memories and understandings whose roots go deep and wide. This grounding will hold the child in good stead, and give her or him a balance—a strength built upon things old, and wise, and true. This they can draw upon throughout their lives, as their grandparents did before them, and their own parents did, too.

Sweetwater Island, August 19

I did the wash today. Not an extraordinary event these days—even for a male. Afterwards, I hung the wash out to dry, which *was* unusual for me. That's something I can't do in the heart of New York City where I live. I wouldn't, even if I could: the air. I could have used the clothes dryer, but the dryer at the cottage we rent here on Sweetwater Island in southeastern Maine is too noisy; it goes on forever, a sixty-minute hyper-buzz that smothers the quiet of this most serene point on the island. I hesitated, though, I have to admit. Hanging out the wash takes time. With the dryer, you just push a button, and you walk away. But the desire for stillness prevailed over laziness. I took the heavy, damp clothes to the back porch and began pinning them to the line. This line is as bowed as a very pregnant cat. It climbs about thirty feet on a slant, nearly touching some rocks along the way, until it reaches its twin pole on a rise. I had previously used it only to hang a bathing suit or two to dry, nothing more.

What this did, this hanging out of the wash, was to give me the sheer satisfaction of completing a domestic task, a satisfaction similar to that Thoreau describes in *Walden* after sweeping out his cabin. It is a domestic task still performed in many parts of the world, if not here, and one that connects you to the old, simple pattern of life. But this did something else, something unexpected. It opened a chest-full—or rather a hamper-full—of memories that had been in profoundly deep storage in my heart. It took me back to Virginia Beach, Virginia where I grew up. More specifically, it took me to 1955, and to my backyard. And in this backyard, my mother was hanging out the wash, and I was there, watching her. My mother, dead these four years now.

Yes, suddenly, there she was. I was, too. I was myself as a boy. I was watching my mother work. I was watching her doing something she had to do at least three or four times a week. She was hanging out the wash to dry: providing clean clothes for her three children, and for her husband, and for herself. She worked efficiently, reaching above her and pinning the edges of the garments to the clothesline. She had two or three wooden pins in her mouth at the ready, replenished steadily from an arsenal in her apron pockets.

She must be thirty-five or thirty-six. She is energetic and real and beautiful. I want to speak to her, but she doesn't like talking when she is hanging out the wash. She doesn't like doing the wash, period. I remember her telling me so, and she wants to finish it as quickly as possible.

Everything about washing clothes and hanging them out to dry in Virginia Beach in 1955 comes back to me on that Maine hill. I know there is a big difference between my hanging out the wash here in Maine and my mother's inescapable routine of long, long ago. I remember driving in the car with her, and seeing it start to rain, and she, full of things in her head, slapping the wheel lightly and saying, "Oh, God, the wash!" She knew the distance between her and the clothes was too great to retrieve them before it poured. So she knew the clothes were out there, getting soaked, getting heavier and heavier, even dragging themselves to the earth and into pools of water made by the rain. No dryers then—at least not for us. What should have been a sure thing was not, and had to be done all over again, with the added work of wringing out the drenched clothes, piece by piece.

I watched her as long as I could today, my Mommy, so alive before me I could hardly believe it. I continued watching her as I pinned my clothes to the more deeply bowing line. I pinned shirts, socks, towels and jeans for my own six year-old daughter, and for me. But even then I could see my mother turn and look at me as I extravagantly used two, sometimes three, clothespins for each piece of laundry. "Double up on those clothespins, Richie!" She meant that two pieces of laundry could share the same pin. You get more on the line then, and the hanging will be over faster.

So there she was, my mother, my faraway gone mother. I could see her again as I had as a ten year-old: my coping—not always coping—mother. She who was to have so many problems and pains later, whose heart was broken and who attempted to repair it with drink. She was mine, and I was hers, for a moment—for an eternity. I think that could only have happened to me here, on Sweetwater Island, where the old verities of life are championed. These are the things which link us to the past and to people who, though dead and far gone, we will always love and try very hard never to forget. And I won't forget you, Mommy.

Sweetwater Island, August 20

The house we rent has a two-sided, expansive porch. We spend a good deal of time on that porch. It faces an exposed eastern point of Sweetwater Island, and so we and the island's weather—which is the fullest here—are pretty well acquainted. Near the house is a small cluster of pine trees. Sometimes for shade, and for peace, I walk into these woods. They are quite different from the dark, Frostian woods that take up most of the center of Sweetwater Island. While you do find shade, you find space and light, too, and soft brown pine needles underfoot. These pines remind me of the pine trees I used to walk among in France, near the Mediterranean.

On the edge of this little cluster of trees, my brother-in-law put up a hammock between two crabapple trees last year. He can lay there, a concave lump, happily reading his French books for hours.

I don't always get the peace I'm after, however. I keep forgetting that in this little woods reside a small, secretive band of crows. When I walk into the trees, more often than not three or four crows suddenly alight, cawing an alert. I jump—their actions are so abrupt. They, of course, had noticed me immediately through the branches. When I come too close for comfort, they start crying bloody murder. If that weren't enough, two or three crows typically remain behind. Without warning, there is a second explosive fleeing and cawing. I jump again. Do they think this is funny?

Through the branches, I see the second group fly away. They are large birds. I can even hear their wings wafting the air. No creature can expose you like a crow. They expose you so blatantly that you feel totally isolated, as if they'd somehow drawn a circle around you. Their caws sound as if they are communicating precisely what color your hair is, how tall you are, how much you weigh, exactly where you are standing, and why you are here. And how obvious you are.

You cannot, on the other hand, surprise a crow.

As long as I've been coming to Sweetwater Island, these crows—or a similar group—have resided here. Last year, they were extremely loud in the early morning. Their caws have the insistence and penetratingness of car alarms. They woke us with their 5 AM bickering and squawking, and I began to have detailed poisoning fantasies. Given half the chance, I would have carried them out. But that would have been very un-Sweetwater Island-like.

This year, thankfully, they seem to be doing their dawn cawing elsewhere—specifically, a few houses down, in front of Helen Colby's cottage. I mean to ask Helen if she has thought of doing away with them. They still retreat to our little woods from time to time, though.

Crows are the most inscrutable of birds—maybe of all animals. They are aloof and secretive, and they exist in their aloof secretiveness almost everywhere on the earth. Crows will be on Sweetwater Island as long as we are, and probably forever. They are the part of a world we will never know, and will never have dominion over. There is a kind of contentment in that.

New York City, May 18

I won't be going to Maine this year. My ex-wife and my daughter will. In the aftermath of divorce, I drifted away from the island, like a boat untied. This always seems to happen after the sundering of a marriage. Common friends are no longer common. Who was originally whose friend becomes clear again through what was once the opaqueness of joint living. Maine was not mine first. It was my wife's. It was she who introduced me to Sweetwater Island. She had gone to college with a woman whose family owned a house—three houses, in fact, on SI, as they call it. She had been going to the island for twenty years, since her college days, and it is part of her. It's part of my daughter, now, too, and I am extremely grateful for that. Maine, especially the islands of Maine, is about as timeless a place you can find.

I'll miss the island, that goes without saying. I'll especially miss those things my daughter and I would do together—*our* things. When she was three, I began taking her out to look for blackberries. I would hold her in one arm as we went from bush to bush searching for the berries, which are often in lovely clusters. Few things are as nourishing to the soul as a Maine-grown blackberry. (For us, the renowned blueberries are a distant second prize.) I remember the time my girl took her first bite. She had a look on her face that you could say was an exclamation mark. Customarily, whenever we would get anything to eat, she would say to me, sometimes sternly, "Save some for Mommy!" After we had gathered a handful of black treasure, I said to her, "Let's save some for Mommy."

"No," she said unemotionally, gathering the blackberries from my palm.

I won't be collecting mussels with her, either. When the tide waned, baring great stretches of soggy land, we would set out on our hunt. There were so many mussels! She loved ripping them from their rocky declivities, running to toss them into a bucket and dashing back for more. She was unquenchable.

"Look, Daddy!" She would rush up with a clump of the black-bearded mollusk in her two hands, hold them up before me, then toss them into the bucket and run back to her spot. I have had few moments as a father as intense as those, with pride and love and mystery coursing through me. Seeing my girl there, her hands and feet slathered in mud, her legs streaking with Maine water, her hair a windy mess, I knew she was fully in her childhood. I knew this was childhood as it's supposed to be. We gathered mussels and gathered. We never fatigued.

"Look, Daddy, over *here*!" she cried to me. We covered the whole mudflat, and then we branched out this way and that. No mussel escaped our relentless pursuit. We were mussel bloodhounds. The good thing about mussels is that you need a lot of them if you're going to cook them. And we were. One person can easily eat twenty. That means you have to collect a lot. The meat itself, just one bite, really, is subtle and delicious. I like the taste Maine mussels better than clams, better than scallops, better than oysters, even better than lobster.

So, we kept looking, the two of us. We got maybe fifty, sixty—even seventy, who knows? It was only the clock that stopped us. We had to take them up to the house, clean them, and cook them. People were coming over for dinner to eat them. Cleaning mussels takes forever, and my girl is not interested in something that takes forever. So, she left the task to me. She doesn't much like eating mussels, either. Never mind. Now my daughter, New York City born and bred, knows what a mussel in the wild looks like, where it comes from, how it lives. She has seen its habitat, and the strength such a small thing can summon to remain in place. She has witnessed how a creature has, with nature's wonderfully bizarre logic, adapted itself to its environment. She has *seen* how suited mussels are to where they live, how suited they are to great tides and to rocks and to microscopic meals. Seeing this amazing compatibility, she will learn to respect that. She will realize how much wiser it is than the things we humans engineer and cry out so loud about. Look, we made a bridge! We shout. My daughter can point and shout, look! Nature made a mussel!

I taught her to climb the rough rocks that jut out from much of the island. I taught her to scamper, to pull, to leap goat-like, and, trickiest of all, to descend. She fell once, in her arrogance. My heart leapt, but she escaped with tears and a little blood. She is daring, and passionately self-sufficient, and you can't stop her. I just pray she won't break her neck. That's one thing the island provides—an opportunity for my daughter to test herself. To discover that she has power within her to surmount difficulties of a physical nature. She is aware now that nature will never go easy on her, just because she is who she is. She is learning that nature is democratic in its indifference. This lesson, and others about the sanctity of our earth, will help connect her with the rest of the world.

She leaves in just a few months. I feel a lump in my throat already. I'll find it very hard to say goodbye to her this time.

Maine, watch over her.

The Bicycle Diaries

Shortly after September 11, 2001, I began riding my bicycle down from my apartment on the Upper West Side in New York City to the World Trade Center disaster site—or as near as I could get to it. I rode down almost every day, in all weather, for about three months. When I came home, I wrote about what I saw.

***

September 11, 2001

When I crossed Madison Avenue on the way to work, I looked south and I saw one of the World Trade Towers bellowing smoke. The other Tower hadn't been hit yet. I could time my position in time by that moment, like the frozen clock at Hiroshima. Smoke was gushing out of the east side of the building. The building was hemorrhaging smoke in a fat black plume. It was as if an aorta running through it had been severed. The smoke was pouring from at least four or five floors. The air was so pure and crystalline that morning, I could see that even from four or five miles away. Anyone who saw it knew that this was no ordinary fire. The building had plainly been grievously wounded, and it was terrifying to see it bleeding so profusely. Even so, no one, in his or her wildest dreams would have thought the wound was mortal.

What was this? People on the street were saying that a plane had crashed into the Tower. What kind of plane? How? No one knew the full truth yet.

I went to my job, and that's when I discovered what had happened. Everyone had seen the news on the Internet. Women were walking up and down the halls crying, just like the day Kennedy was assassinated. I tried to call my former wife, Brenda Bowen, at Simon & Schuster where she worked. I couldn't get through. I sent her an e-mail, but had no idea if that made it through. I tried to call our daughter's school, which was, I thanked God, far to the north, at 114th Street, on the West Side of Manhattan. I couldn't get through.

I left. There was no reason to stay.

I re-crossed Madison again, looked south, and saw the building was still burning, but in my hurry to find my ex-wife and my daughter, I don't remember seeing both of the towers burning, or if one of them had fallen. Everyone was walking—the whole city, it seemed. The streets were full of people walking. They were walking quickly, with an urgency. Everyone was trying to get home, wherever that was. They flowed off the sidewalks and into the streets. No one could get a cab, the busses were full, and it seemed insane to go into the subway. The only option was to walk.

It was a sunny, a brilliant day—I will never forget how beautiful and lucid the day was—an easy day to walk great distances. I asked to borrow a cell phone from someone, but most cell phones weren't working, and this one didn't either. The lines at the public phones were six or seven deep. I wanted to get to Simon & Schuster to find Brenda, and to see if she was all right, and to make sure our daughter was ok. No one knew anything then, you have to remember.

The guard at Simon & Schuster told me Brenda had left already. I began my walk to the Upper West Side, to home. (I lived two blocks from Brenda at the time.) I finally found a phone that worked and got through at least to Brenda's answering machine. I told her I was ok, said I hoped she was, and that I was going to the school to find out about our daughter. "Leave a message," I said. "If you get this, let me know if you're all right. God bless our daughter," I said. This was a day that unsettled our very cores, that uprooted us from all our connections.

It was strangely peaceful as I made my way up Riverside Drive that morning. There were a few people walking along with me. Everyone's pace was fast. I finally reached my ex-wife on the telephone. She said she was all right and that she had been to the school already and that our daughter was ok. The head of the school had told the parents they could take their child home, but she recommended they leave them in school for a sense of normalcy.

I went to the school myself, saw the head of school, and heard it from her lips, and felt she was right. I went back to Brenda's apartment. We were thankful we were both all right. We looked at one another as so many others that day in New York did, with a deep sense of fearful disbelief. What had they done to our city? What had happened to us? We knew so little. It wasn't even noon yet.

September 13, 2001

I couldn't stand being in front of the television anymore. I was watching what was going on just a few miles to the south, and it seemed that I was protecting myself from the terror in my own city. It seemed that I should at least try to get closer to this terrible scene where so many New Yorkers had died. I got my bicycle, and at around 7PM took off south on the long pathway that runs adjacent to the Hudson River on the west side of Manhattan. It is a beautiful pathway, used by joggers and bicyclists, and you can practically touch the river. You feel the smell of water, a breeze, and there are no buildings, just boats and water. The sun was just setting, and it was a beautiful sunset, fiery orange on a lovely evening. I thought of how those killed would never see a sunset again. Then all sorts of never-again scenarios taxed my mind.

I rode south on the path by the river to 59th Street where police stopped me. (The path continues all the way to the foot of Manhattan and runs close by the World Trade Center.) They weren't New York police; at least I didn't recognize the uniform. This was to be the first of many encounters with policemen from other parts of the state and from neighboring states. I rode my bike to the east side of the highway and went unhindered until I came to the Javits Center, an enormous dark glass building at 34th Street and 12th Avenue that is used normally for conventions.

There was an amazing scene. Hundreds of people—workers—were standing around waiting to be transported to the disaster area. It looked like a mass of humanity about to enter a professional football game; there were that many, and they were that concentrated. I spoke to one highway patrolman who said they weren't taking people downtown, because the area had been closed. Too dangerous. I asked if he'd been. "Yeah. Twice. But it was stupid. First five minutes I was there someone pushed me out of the way and a huge glass window fell and just missed me. Me, a highway patrolman. What the hell am I doing there?"

I biked on south, and then the scene took on an eerie, warlike scene. It was dark now. The highway was completely clear except for official vehicles, and they were racing both south and north, sirens screaming, lights flashing. Sometimes four, five, six cars and vans would rush by in a group, other times a single unmarked car would fly by, the inside red bulb flashing, its siren wailing. Those moving away from the disaster scene moved with as much urgency and speed as those moving toward the scene. At Chelsea Piers—a sports complex on the river at 23rd street—I saw at least twenty ambulances parked one after another, engines off, just waiting. There were from everywhere—Passaic, Elizabeth, other towns in New Jersey, Long Island, Nyack, even Boston. Ambulance after ambulance. Fifteen brand-new NYPD tow trucks zoomed by in a tight line, heading south in a formation as precise as any military convoy.

Everything on the highway moved at high speed, whether it was an unmarked police car, a phone company van, or a sanitation truck. A single tow truck came north towing a NYPD police car that was covered in a perfect coat of white ash. Someone had likened the disaster scene to Pompeii because of the ash covering everything, and this car made the disaster seem particularly immediate.

Still the cars and vans and trucks kept coming with an unrelenting insistency. The number of vehicles, the logistics, the coordination of it, the sheer scope of it was immense, massive, enormous. Vehicles of every type moving every direction and flawlessly, as if this reaction to disaster had been mapped out to the last detail years ago and rehearsed many times over. No vehicle got in another vehicle's way. Only sirens wailed, no horns honked. So unlike New York, no horns. Everything moved with great speed. It seemed as if New York had become a country, an independent country, with its own army, navy, and chief of state. The resources were astonishing. I had to see it to believe it. And I didn't even approach the disaster scene.

At 14ᵗth Street, I couldn't go further. I had to have had an ID demonstrating I lived in the area in order to pass the State Police who manned those barricades. I rode back to the West Side Highway. Along the side of the road forty or fifty people cheered each time a rescue vehicle came from the scene—whether it was a fire truck, police car, or a sanitation truck—any moving vehicle. They held up signs: "You're our heroes." I stopped and applauded, too. The drivers flying by would honk their horns in response appreciatively. But you couldn't see their faces; they were going too fast.

September 15, 2001

Humankind cannot bear very much reality, as T.S. Eliot said, and that's certainly true for me, here and now. It's true of everyone now, I'm sure. Yet I can't help but write about the things I saw today. It was, thankfully, a beautiful day, cool and sunny, with little wind. The kind of day that does not add to the oppressiveness of labor. I wanted to donate the things I wasn't able to donate yesterday—men's and women's underwear, and batteries—comical, but they were on the *Supplies List for World Trade Center Disaster As of 9/13/01* I picked up near Chelsea Piers the other day. (Food was handled elsewhere.) Here are some of the items they asked for:

Aspirin
Respirator Masks
Saline Solution (Highly Needed)
Non-drowsy Allergy Medicine
Butterfly (To Draw Blood)
Dog Food
Can Openers
Multi-channel, 2-way radios
Sanitary Napkins
Steel-toed Work Boots
Crowbars
Hard Hats
Packaged Ice
High Quality Respirators
Dusk Masks

Foot Powder
23 Gauge Needles
Dog Boots (Canine Unit)
Shovels
Tents (All Kinds)
Sunscreen
Rope
Pick Axes
Handi-Wipes
Plastic Tarps

    I took the same bike route south from 103rd Street along the Hudson as I did Thursday. I fairly flew. The bicycle, somehow, seemed to give what I was doing a sense of meaning. I don't know why.

    When I arrived, the Javits Center was crowded. I gave my things to a woman, and stayed for a while. I talked with a man who had been at the disaster site. He had been trying to get back, but couldn't. He said what everyone else has said after they've been there: "It's impossible to describe." He'd slept on the sidewalk the previous night, as had many others. A young woman came by taking names and addresses of people who would let workers sleep at their apartments—or just take a shower. I gave her mine. (I never got a call.) She asked a woman more near my age near me the same questions. The woman looked horrified.

    "I live in Westchester. I...I'll have to call my husband."

    "I have a cell phone," the young woman immediately said. "You can call him now."

    "Uh...I...ah...just called him. He's not home."

    The young woman shrugged. I looked at the Westchester woman who had slithered her way out of this basic act of generosity. Well, I was glad—and it didn't surprise me—that she was from Westchester, not from New York.

    I lingered a bit, but it was time to leave. I wanted to see if today I could get closer, close enough, to the tragedy itself. I left, turned back onto the West Side Highway, and biked south.

    When I got to 14th street, I saw no policemen manning barricades. I knew that the mayor had opened up the area, as he said he would do, south to Canal Street. He was intent on returning things, if not to normalcy, then to routine. Where I live—103rd

Street—is about eight or nine miles north of the World Trade Center. 14th Street is about two to three miles north, and Canal Street is about a mile. I turned my bike onto 14th Street from the West Side Highway, and I banked right onto Washington Street. I lived for twelve years on 12th Street and Hudson Street, which is not far away. From biking those many years, I knew the entire area south of 14th Street extremely well. So, I purposely turned onto Washington Street, because I knew it lead directly, and uninterruptedly, to the World Trade Center.

Normally, when I bike down Washington Street, I have an unobstructed view of the Twin Towers. In fact, it's a wonderful, almost private view. Particularly on weekends, this street is not heavily traveled. Around Houston Street, the Towers loom extremely large in the near distance. On a Sunday morning, it's an incomparable New York experience. Now, here's what television could not begin to relate. I looked, and I thought—quite honestly and reflexively—that my eyes were deceiving me. I said, "My eyes must be deceiving me," reflexively mouthing this cliché. The Towers were gone. It was as some illusionist had made the Twin Towers vanish in a great feat of prestidigitation, and I was part of the astonished audience. I looked intently. They weren't there. Where were they?

Something was amiss with my mental process. Perhaps it wasn't Washington Street that used to give me such a good view of the Twin Towers. Perhaps I was wrong. After all, I hadn't biked down this street in a while. I should try another street, I thought. But I could see smoke in the distance, a fat white cloud of smoke slowly and continually rising where the towers were, or once were. My eyes were not deceiving me, though it was difficult to believe.

I rode very quickly. Any other day, I would have been exhilarated by the ride. I passed across Houston Street and came to Canal Street. All the streets flowing south of Canal were barricaded and manned by police. This was now the line of demarcation. Canal Street is a major thoroughfare in lower Manhattan. It cuts across the island, starting from the Hudson River on the west, goes east to Chinatown, and then flows into the Manhattan Bridge and over to Brooklyn on the east side. But more important, it branches directly to the Holland Tunnel, one of two tunnels that go from Manhattan to New Jersey. These tunnels were now heavily guarded. There they were, the police. The fact was, if you lived south of Canal Street, and you had ID proving it, they let you in. If you didn't, they turned you away. I did not, and they wouldn't let me in.

I decided to lie. It seemed a bit filthy, but I decided to do it anyway. I needed to see what was down there. It was *my* city. They had hurt *my* city. But how could I get in without ID? Too many years of soaking up the demiworld of New York City gave me an idea. I told them I was a painter. I told them that while I lived on the Upper West Side, my studio was south of Canal, in Tribeca. This is where a lot of painters have studios, and even cops know this. I told them I had an ID saying that I lived on Riverside Drive, but, unfortunately, I had nothing on me showing my Tribeca studio address. The police were very solicitous, but it didn't work at the first two checkpoints. I biked east toward Chinatown, and my ruse worked at the Avenue of the Americas.

"Where is your studio exactly?" the policeman asked me. Jesus Christ. Where was it? "It's at Duane and Chambers," I said. That is fairly south of Canal and not too far from the World Trade Center. I didn't want to give him an address just a block or two south, because that would have been useless.

"Ok," the policeman said. "You can go, but I don't know how far you'll get. They're a lot stricter as you go further south. The army's there."

I went through the gap in the barrier. The Avenue of Americas runs north, and so I was riding against traffic, but that didn't matter. There was no traffic. The whole scene suddenly felt different. There was an aura to everything, which I can't explain, a disquieting, quiet aura. I was surprised to see how many gas company trucks were along the way with men digging into the streets.

I got as far south as Reade Street, which is probably only a half mile from the World Trade Center. There were about twenty people there, along with TV trucks with satellite dishes. The police were no longer in charge. The U.S. Army was. A solider (or a National Guardsman) stopped me and everyone else with an upraised hand. I backed off. I did not want to chance exposing a lie to the military. He had a machine gun.

But I could see what I had come to see. I saw directly ahead of me that fence-like structure of steel of one of the Towers, the jutting, broken comb remnant that everyone saw on TV. And what I could only have realized being there, standing that close, was how enormous that thing was. It was large and broad, even from half a mile away. It stood there with all the brute power of a modern abstract sculpture, except that it was far bigger. And the hugeness of it took my breath away. What seemed so small—a mere puzzle-piece of a remain—hit me in the gut and made me queasy. The enormity of this section opened my eyes as to how huge the towers actually were—as to how much destruction, how enormous the buildings were, how much steel and glass there must have been. This was comparable to the vision you have as to how huge an animal is solely by the size of its footprint.

I began to tremble. I couldn't take in the enormity. The steel remains were in a smoky mist, a leaning grid, and it was too terrible to look at it for too long. I had to leave. I couldn't imagine what courage it took to actually be there.

I rode my bike north and crossed back across Canal—glad now that I was no longer under the pretext of a lie. I went east to Lafayette Street, one of New York's most beautiful big streets. The Public Theatre is on Lafayette Street. The Puck Building—a gem of a dark brick structure—is on Lafayette Street. I love riding it. I was hungry, and got a croissant at a good French bakery, then continued north. But I stopped. I stopped at Ladder 20 Engine 14 Fire Station, which is between Spring and Prince, just south of Houston Street. I had seen the station many times, because in another one of my lives in New York, I had lived on Crosby Street, which is the next street over from Lafayette, and my apartment looked out directly on to the station. It was familiar in an eerie way. I stopped, because I saw bundles and bundles of flowers and wreaths placed before the front of the station's entranceway, and candles burning, and notes of appreciation.

There were a few firemen milling about inside, but not many. I was reluctant to approach any of them. Everyone knows by now that 343 firemen lost their lives the day of the disaster. 343! As the *Times* put it so well, "Firefighters stand apart from the rest of us, simply by the fact that they are trained to run toward a blaze and not away from it. That impulse, which amounts to a special vocation, is their greatest tool in protecting their communities. On Tuesday that learned instinct drew many of them into the World Trade Center at a time when the burning fuel from two crashed jetliners was creating heat that could buckle steel. There were people in those buildings, and the firefighters went to get them. The losses were staggering."

Despite my reluctance, I stayed for a few minutes, trying to garner the courage to speak to one of the firemen. Then I saw, just inside of the stationhouse, one of those white message boards you write on with crayon and can erase later. On it was written:

Pray for

Larry
Andy
Billy
John
Timmy
Eric
Manny
Dave
Bobby
John
Jimmy
Sean
Bob
Dave

Fourteen men.

I finally mustered the courage to talk to one of the men in the stationhouse. "Those men," I asked him, pointing to the board, "they're all missing?"

He nodded, but then he said evenly, "Well, not all of them are missing anymore."

I was reading Gerard Manley Hopkins' poem "The Wreck of the Deutschland" last night trying to get sense and solace. No one ever struggled more valiantly and directly with the mystery of tragedy than he, and this poem is about the destruction in a gale of a ship bound for America, and of those who drowned. Two lines he wrote stood out, one perhaps appropriate for this whole tragedy: "I am soft sift / In an hourglass." The other for the list of men in the firehouse, and for all the lists all around the city: "Hope had grown gray hairs."

    I walked away. I was weeping. Nearby, on a sort of makeshift wire stand to the left of the entranceway, was a single pair of fireman's boots, bent, smothered in ashes, empty.

When I'm Sixty-Four

One day, things begin to change. You don't remember exactly when, but they do. You start getting out of bed a little slower, and a little more reluctantly. You find yourself moving toward the bathroom a bit unsteadily, and your back is creaking like an old floor. You look at yourself in the mirror and you see a stranger. Who the hell is that frightening-looking man? How did he get in the house? I don't know him. I wish he would go away. He's old.

Suddenly you have skin hanging under your chin like a suspension bridge. Hair grows out of your nose and ears like spring corn, and your eyebrows start looking like Bertrand Russell's. Let's not forget the encroaching gauntness that slowly but surely makes you look like you've just been liberated from Bataan. And stairs missed, names forgotten, routines ferociously protected, and the more frequent trips to the pharmacy.

Getting old.

Getting old, and with it, so many new ways the world looks at me, and I at the world.

I'm getting the sense of what having a disfigured face is like. I'm beginning to see certain reactions to my own. It's nothing like poor Lucy Greely got, but I still think the analogy works. Inside, I'm young and eager and robust. But the face I show to the world doesn't mirror this energetic youth I am inside. A woman I know who's my age—which is sixty, by the way—put it this way. "I feel like I'm in disguise," she said.

This inside/outside disparity has forced me to make adjustments to the way I behave. If I see a pretty woman—not nineteen, but a reasonable age, say thirty-five or forty—inside, I'm bounding after her, a swain struck by her beauty who wants to declare his admiration. If those feelings transfer to the look on my face, though, I can get into trouble. I have to remember this is the face of a sixty-year-old man.

Sometimes, I do forget, and I can see those subtle reactions of impropriety on the woman's face. I don't know why the woman is looking at me this way, her eyes beginning to avert. Then I'll pass by a store window and see my reflection and think, Oh, no, she was reacting to the outside me, not to the inside me, not to the *real* me. And I want to run after her and say, "Miss, you mustn't get the wrong idea. It was the *real* me who was admiring you, the me that's as young as you are. I'm not old, for God's sake. This face is not me. It's fake. I wish I could take it off and show you. I'm not *really* sixty! Can you understand that?" I never do this, of course, because it would only be a matter of time before I was carted off to jail or to the lunatic asylum.

Then Faustian thoughts begin to crowd my mind.

Living where I do, in New York City near Columbia University, where there is a constant ebb and flow of youth, makes me think dark thoughts indeed. I start to have covetous rants in my mind, the kind you hear old men make to themselves under their breath in scary movies. Why should *they* be young, I think, and *I* be growing old? Why should *they* have their life ahead of them, and I have mine mostly behind me? I—I who would know how to use their youth to its fullest degree—I should have their youth.

I want your youth, I think, *you* there, bright savage boy, with your studied insouciance, flip-flops, tousled hair, tattoo, and torn T-shirt. I covet what you have, and *I'm going to have it.* In the dark of the night I'll come to your dorm room and threading my way among beer cans, your baseball glove, lacrosse stick, assorted balls, X-box, bong, condoms, bottles of booze, female clothing left behind, fraternity paddle, the seventies outfit you wore to a "pimps 'n' hos" party and unopened textbooks, I'll come to you while you're sleeping. Then I'll sink my teeth into your neck, and I'll suck your blood. I'll imbibe your youth, drain it from your body. I'll feel its strength shoot through my own veins, replenishing me. Then I'll leave you there, with two tiny denture marks on your neck.

I shudder to think of the indignities that lie in wait for me, ready to crush me like a California mudslide. It's all there in the look of utter terror old people have when you approach them on the street. As they raise their heads slowly from their bent-over positions, or from their walkers, to look at you, their eyes seem to say, "Help me. Please. Rescue me."

In looking forward, I also look back. I look back at the youthful me. I smile, and I wince as well. I see this young Richard making mistakes, wounding people, sometimes deeply and cruelly. I see him cheating on his girlfriend, who was so kind and openhearted. I see him lying to people who mattered in his life. I see moments when he could have reached out his hand and not given in to fear. But he did give in, and he left undone those things he ought to have done. I see him missing opportunities to be closer to his brother and the gap ever widening between these two men, like a departing boat and land. I hear words unspoken that should have been spoken, clearly and bravely.

But I'm also saying good-bye to a young man who was as cocky as Walt Whitman, as wondrous, as capable of inhaling this intense world, desirous of making meaning of it, of giving gifts to it. And he did; he gave freely without stinting, everything that he had. The best of him. I see him drinking in life in deep, indiscriminate gulps. I'm also saying good-bye to that laugh he had, so robust and so freely given, exploding into the air and giving buoyancy to everyone around him. I'm saying good-bye to the me in the full measure of my powers, to those days when I was on a pinnacle, when I could see forever, work forever, dream forever. When I was exploding with energy, boundless in energy, with energy to spare, with energy to share with other countries, other planets, other galaxies. Here, take some, go warm your cold planet with this superfluous energy of mine. Take it.

I see him, and I want to say to him, "Yes, do that! Go ahead! *Don't* be afraid! And for God's sake, write. Write more! Write your heart out, write until your eyes are blurry and your breath is short. Write as if you were going to die the next day or, better, the next hour. Listen to me, Richard, I know what's ahead. Please—listen. Why are you hesitating? I know how little time there is. You won't get it back. It's exhaustible. It runs out. It does run out. Go—open that door. Board that plane. Write that sentence."

But he doesn't listen, this Richard. He won't do what I tell him to do. He never did. I know that.

Do I have to say good-bye to that man?

I saw my Aunt Constance not too long ago. This is a woman who for my entire life, perhaps more than anyone else, has represented adulthood and being old to me. She always looked old, even when she was relatively young. In that sense, she always seemed alien to me, like someone from another world. She's a very strange woman who has said wildly inappropriate things her entire life. She had Tourette's syndrome long before it was fashionable. At a sixtieth birthday dinner some people gave for me, she managed to sit next to me, nearly pushing someone over in the process. "Here I am!" she said, giggling. Midway through the meal, she stopped eating, leaned over, and peered at me closely. Then she said, very deliberately, "Richie, I never thought I'd live to see you as an old man."

No, Constance, no. Not me. You must have the wrong man.

My Beautiful Ann

"You need to explore your Jewish roots!" Ann Silberling was saying this to me—yet again. How many times had she admonished me to do this? Once I'd told her that I was half-Jewish, and she jumped on that confession like a cat on a moving piece of string. She never let go.

"I think this may be the reason you're having some of the problems you are," she said.

"*Like what?*" I asked, a bit defensively, but curious.

"I don't know. But that's why you need to explore your Jewish roots—to find out."

"But I'm not interested in exploring my Jewish roots."

"How do you know?" She was walking from her kitchen to the soft, formal chair she preferred to address me from.

"I just do. I feel Christian. That's the way I was raised."

"I think you're afraid to." She sat down deep into her chair.

I couldn't help but heed that reedy, Manhattan voice, rising in pitch to make this statement nearly a question. Ann's voice had shadings that suited the moment, and, if the moment got serious, it descended into a mellow, oboe-like tone. I couldn't convince her that I wasn't at all curious about that fifty percent of my blood supply and DNA that came from Jews. Ann shrugged her shoulders, one slightly more cocked than the other.

"All right," she said. "All right. But," she raised a defiant index finger, "I think you're avoiding something."

"Maybe. Maybe I'll look into it one day."

"Yeah, right."

I was seated on the couch of her apartment at 302 West 12th Street in Greenwich Village, that storied and still gorgeous commonwealth in lower New York City. Normally when people use that expression, "Yeah, right," I'm slightly annoyed. It seems to indicate, "*I'll* be the one to decide whether or not this is true." But I was never bothered when Ann said it. With her, it seemed as natural as rain. We had become friends when I lived on the same floor as she at 302 West, a large, wonderful, pre-war building on the western edge of Greenwich Village. I stayed in touch when I moved to the Upper West Side. I loved to visit her. I had spent many an hour in her apartment before I left, and I wanted to remain friends. I tried to visit her at least once a month, sometimes more, usually by bicycling down from my apartment. She was my rabbi, my guru, my priest.

At the time I am writing about, in the fall of 1990, Ann was seventy-eight years old. But a strong seventy-eight. I was forty-five. She was always a resourceful, independent woman, and ever more so at that age. She was short, not precisely squat, but nearly so, with thickish arms. She had curly auburn hair that was slowly turning to white, and the pale skin that accompanies that hair color. She dressed very elegantly, in a conservative way, as a select group of older New York City women do. There is a certain type of older Manhattan woman—and I've encountered many of them in my three decades here—not rich, who are widowed, or divorced, or who never married, who live alone with enough money to get by well enough in this city that does not treat those that just scrape by with much decency. They give the place a consistent dignity by their dress, decorum, and demeanor. They demand respect, and by their savvy, grace, and deep understanding of how to encounter New York City, they get it. Ann was one of these women. Her apartment was well turned out, not extravagant, but furnished with a lifetime of carefully acquired mementos—artwork from vacations taken in cities and islands; photos of nieces and nephews and their children; books; vases; various miniature ceramic holders of some arcane craft, ashtrays no longer used but at the ready. It was difficult to find a space upon which something wasn't *placed*.

As I say, she dressed well, and conservatively. Skirts, always to below the knee. It was cotton in the summer, and wool in the winter. She had a sharp eye for color, especially in the summer when I would be surprised and delighted to see her in a soft, peach-hued dress, flowing, and pretty. But never sexy! No, no. She wore those blue and white Chanel scarves with the key and lock-like logo, often in an ascot. She wore a sweater in both summer and winter, a cardigan. She might have a pin or brooch affixed on the sweater, perhaps something she bought at the Metropolitan Museum of Art Gift Shop, where she volunteered. She wore cotton or silk blouses, buttoned almost to the neck. But don't let that give you the impression she was stuffy or formal. Far from it. A visit to Ann's was a klatsch, a not-quite-mad tea party, a two-person salon. We could talk about anything. Ann had heard it all.

    I lived for eleven years on the same floor as she in 302 West, and that's where I got to know her. That floor! What an odd assortment of characters, like the most imaginative human Whitman's Sampler box. Across from my apartment were an actress and her boyfriend who argued as erotically as Stella and Stanley. Next to me was a loopy, misanthropic man who had been raised in that apartment and stayed after his parents moved to Florida. He had never lived anywhere else since he was a baby. Now, he was in his forties, and lived alone. Down the hall, a mournful-looking Jewish doctor from Argentina, not so old, but who no longer practiced medicine because of a heart condition. Then Ann. Then a television producer and his ethereal wife, whom I shamelessly desired. And then, at the end of the hall, a middle-aged lesbian couple, shy and private, both whom Ann and I were fond of. Ann knew them all. I didn't. I was more standoffish. Not so Ann. People felt at ease around her. People talked to her, they opened to her. She listened, and she noted. She broke through my own special brand of xenophobia, simply by being Ann Silberling. Gradually, we became friends. I visited her apartment, she mine.

    Ann was in many ways the quintessential New Yorker. She was Jewish. Oh, yes! With a name like Silberling, what would you expect? She grew up in a family of ten children on the Lower East Side—a Lower East Side that I thought had long vanished, one right out of Henry Roth's gorgeous web of a novel, *Call It Sleep*. Her parents spoke Yiddish almost exclusively, and, in fact, knew little English. They could function perfectly well in their neighborhood, though. Her mother couldn't read or write. She was born in a small farming village in Poland. Ann was very proud of her. Her mother managed to raise ten children, and all of them went to college. Think of it! This all seemed to me as romantic a notion as a woman living in a sod house on the Nebraskan prairie whose children went to Princeton.

Ann had a secret. Deep, not so dark, but dark enough for her. And I didn't know it at the time.

I didn't go to Ann's apartment only to gossip, but, I have to admit, I liked it when we did. She had unrivaled intelligence about the building, and not just about her—and my former—floor. Everybody seemed to tell her everything. She knew the most intimate details about people. When I came to visit her from my apartment on the Upper West Side, I loved to have a rundown on the denizens of my old building.

"Did you know Bernice Savage," Ann asked, giving up trying to get me to explore my Jewish roots—for the time being.

"Uh...."

"You know. She was always with whaddayacallit that company downtown. Always wore those blue men's shirts."

"Oh, yes! I remember. I always thought she was gay."

"She's *not*."

"Not?"

"*No*. I saw her in *Beatrice's* one night, eating alone, and so I asked her if I could join her. She said yes. I found out so much about her I never knew." She had that delectable revelatory tone of gossip in her voice.

"Such as?" I leaned forward.

"Such as—she's got a boyfriend."

"No."

"*Yes*. Apparently she's his mistress."

"What?" Much later, I was to return, in my mind, to this revelation.

"*Yes*. But he's very sick now." Her voice took on a tone of concern.

"Oh."

"And so she's a bit depressed."
"Oh, wow, I never would have...."
"Thought. Me either."
"She always looked so dyke-y to me."
"Yeah right. But she's not!"

Today, Ann wore a long summer dress and, because she had the air conditioning on, that white cardigan sweater draped over her shoulders. When I first knew her she had a sweet little French poodle, a stray she had picked up on the side of the road somewhere. When she found her, the dog was filthy, but Ann got that taken care of. She tended that dog, got her washed, clipped, and coiffed. The little dog always looked wonderfully smart and fashionable, always had two pretty pink ribbons in her hair. She was just as much a lady as Ann was. Her name was—well, of course—Gigi. Ann and she were very happy together. I used to go on her walks with Gigi around the neighborhood.

That neighborhood! Abingdon Square and West 12th Street and Bleecker Street and Hudson. Wonderful streets! It includes one of the most enduringly beautiful streets in New York City—West Fourth Street. Oh, that long, slim street, on each bank of which are silent noble brownstones, so inviting to look into. It always has the most gratifying palette of sun and shadow playing across its surface and dappling from the trees that rise along its sides. So we'd walk Gigi in the summer evening or the sharp cool fall days and talk. We'd walk up West Fourth Street past those storied streets that cross it—Charles, Perry and Bank—the little dog sniffing out the landscape haughtily, the bell on her smart collar jangling as she shook her head after smelling something disreputable. Ann loved the street and the neighborhood, as did I. We'd return to her apartment, and she'd make me tea or coffee, sometimes lunch. And we'd visit.

I loved Ann for who she was—she was *fun* to be with. We had many things in common, but perhaps the one overriding commonality was our deep, wide love for New York City. So we would often talk about The City, as New Yorkers call it, in that way that two people from the same foreign country will meet at a party and begin talking in their own language. When Ann and I talked about

New York's personality, we never explained. It didn't matter that we were each preaching to the choir. Preach on!

"You know Essex Street, Ann?" This was an ancient street on the Lower East Side. It was in the heart of old Jewish New York.

"Do I know…of co…listen, I used to go to school, to elementary school, on Essex Street. Do I know Essex Street."

"Ok. I'm assuming you do."

She gave me a half-smile. "You can assume."

"Do you know that store that sells the pickles, the half-sours?"

"Sure—what—I used—my mother used to buy from that store."

"Big fat open barrels. The kind you might find on a pirate ship. Full to the brim with light green pickles!"

"Yeah right."

Oh those pickles. With a pale green color so subtle it might be on a bird's egg. When you bit into them, there was a crisp snap that released their heady briny juices. Those pickles in the open big barrel would take me directly to a place and time of Jews in old New York. Many of the stores nearby had signs in Hebrew or Yiddish—no English—when I first came to New York. This was a way of life. Now it's disappeared. So here we were, two people talking about a vanished world like two ancient Jews on a park bench somewhere. Or a Jew and a half, anyway.

"So what are you writing?" she asked. The last word in that sentence flew upward in the air. It was typical of Ann, this Yiddish-based inflection that gave questions the faintest air of impatience. It implied—at least to me—so why aren't you writing?

"Oh, I'm not doing much. I can't seem to get going. I'm stuck. I'm blocked. It's terrible."

She looked at me knowingly.

"What?"

"I'm not saying anything."

"What?"

"You know."

"*My Jewish roots.*" I parroted.

"It's there somewhere," she said. "Mark my words."

"What—were you a shrink in another life—or a rabbi?"
She laughed. "We did have rabbis in our family."
"Well, it shows."
"Listen," she changed the subject, "I have some paintings here, some watercolors, I don't need. Over there. Go. Look. Why don't you take one?"

Her apartment, as I said, was packed with all sorts of *tchotchkes*. Hardly an inch in her apartment didn't have some sort of *thing* perched on it, or in it. Every time I came, she offered me something that I normally graciously refused to take. Her apartment overlooked Abingdon Square. It faced the Hudson River, west, and so light cascaded in at all seasons. It was cheery even in winter. The kitchen was tiny. In it she made me the occasional omelet and salad for lunch, emerging with plates for each of us. We would sit at her small table at the west-facing windows and eat. It was more appealing than the apartment I used to have on the same floor, which didn't have a view, and was dark. Her bedroom had a large bed and television and one of those pre-war bathrooms with its ancient, massive enamel sink so prized by New Yorkers.

Ann had worked for years for the Board of Education but was retired. She kept herself occupied, though. She worked, as I mentioned, as a volunteer for the Metropolitan Museum of Art, and often when I'd call her up to ask if she wanted a visit, she'd say, "Not today. It's my museum day. Come another time. It would be nice to see you." She went to concerts, to plays, to movies. She had two sisters in New York—some of her ten siblings had died, and others lived away from New York—and she visited them regularly, as well. Also a slew of nieces and nephews and great-nieces and great-nephews she went on about.

"Sharon—my great-niece, my sister's daughter's daughter, who lives in Seattle—she's a writer. And a very good one. She works for whatayacallit some famous magazine. Maybe she can help you with your work. You want me to call her? And my brother's son's wife's cousin is a writer."

I bristled. No! Damn it, I wanted to say. I don't need your niece. I'm just *blocked*. It's not like golf lessons, where you get someone to adjust your swing. But I held my tongue. I had learned a long time ago that most people look upon writing as a pastime and not as real work. Ann was no different than anyone else in this regard.

"You know Silvia from the twelfth floor?" Ann said, after she saw that I was going to decline her offer.

"No."

"You don't? Well, she was here the other night. She has cancer."

"Oh."

"Ovarian." She leaned forward.

"That's not good."

"She had it before. She was in remission. Five years!"

"It's all about luck, isn't it?"

"Yeah, right."

Ann never married. In all the time I knew her—twenty years or so—men were never an issue. I never once heard her wish for a man, or for romance. I did see a large photograph of a man on her wall, though. This intrigued me. It was a black and white photograph. The man was in profile, he looked a bit Roman, with an aquiline nose, nearly bald head, and an intelligent gaze. He looked rugged, but with a curiosity in his eyes, perhaps like an archeologist in the field.

"Who's that?" I asked Ann one day, pointing to the photo, unable to resist.

"Oh him. That's Daniel. That's the man I loved."

"Loved?"

"Well, yes. He's not in my life anymore."

"He's very good looking."

"Yeah, right. I know." She smiled. I'd never seen that smile before! The smile of Eros! Oh, how coy she all of a sudden looked!

"How did you meet him?"

"In Israel."

"Israel? Did you live there?"

"No. I was visiting. But he would come here a lot. And when he did, we got together."

"Long distance."

"Yeah right, but the time we spent together was very special."

I was so happy to hear this! To hear that she had once had these intense feelings coursing through her. But then I wondered. I wondered why this intelligent, humorous and kind woman had lived alone her entire life.

"So...you...never...wanted to get married to him?" I said.

And then I saw something I'd never seen Ann do before. And because of that, I was surprised, even stunned. She blushed. Her face flushed a light crimson, and she lowered her eyes. When she spoke she didn't look directly at me.

"Well," she said softly, "he was married."

She had a "There, I said it" look on her face. Her face was open, exposed, subject to judgment, weak.

"*Ann!*" I said. I couldn't help myself! It was so unlike her! Or what I presumed was her. It was shocking. It was wonderful. Ann. My Ann—a man's *mistress!*

"I know, I know," she said, eyes downcast. Then I could see she was actually ashamed.

"Oh, I didn't mean...look, I'm not judging you! Not that I'd even have a right to."

"Yeah, right. But it's something I'm not proud of."

"Love will make us do most anything." And then I thought of Bernice Savage, how she had been a man's mistress without a soul suspecting.

"I suppose so," she said.

Yes, I thought of Bernice Savage, the woman in the building I thought was gay, and who wasn't, by a long shot. I thought how little we know of the lives of people.

"So, he would come to New York, and you would see him then?"

"Yes."

"For how long?" I felt like I worked for *People Magazine* with these questions. I looked up at the photograph of this Israeli man, who might have been a tank commander, with his warrior aspect, and hauteur, and thought, *They were lovers! Clandestine lovers!*

"We were together for about eight years." She paused. "Then he disappeared."

"He...what?"

"He stopped calling. I don't know why. And that was that."
"Oh, Ann."

She sat there, with Gigi lying on the floor by her side. She shrugged her shoulders. "That's the way life goes sometimes," she said.

What a bastard, I thought. He had awakened passion and love in her—all those powerful good things our bodies and hearts deserve—and then he dropped her. I was angry. But she hadn't taken the photograph down, had she?

I left that day like I'd seen a great play. I was excited and felt, somehow, renewed.

I continued my visits through the years. Often I would get on my bicycle and ride down from my apartment at 103rd Street to the Village. This was always exhilarating. To be flying down the narrow path that runs adjacent to the wide, strong Hudson, smelling fresh, moving water and early-morning scents, uncorrupted by the day, the power of my legs pumping, was to be unmistakably alive. When I'd get to Greenwich Village, and turn down Charles or Perry Street, I'd think: maybe I'll stop and see Ann. Over to 302 West 12th I'd ride. I'd lock my bike in front of that familiar building I still loved and stroll into the lobby. I'd ask the doorman to ring Ann up, and, if she were there, I'd hear that voice crackling through the intercom, "Have him come up!" And up I'd go, to be greeted by Ann and an investigative Gigi. Ann and I talked about anything and everything, and, of course, eventually we'd get around to people in the building and to New York.

I'd gotten married by then and had a daughter. Once, when my girl was six or seven, I brought her with me to meet Ann. I wanted her to know this woman. I wanted her to know someone other than the mothers and fathers of the children in her Upper West Side private school. I wanted her to know this genuine, rare New York woman who had emerged, so wonderfully, from the ancient Lower East Side. She made my daughter her traditional omelet and salad. The three of us sat, and ate, and my daughter was polite and quiet, but I could see she wanted to go off with me. It was too un-kid-like for her. I don't know if she recalls the few visits to Ann's apartment, but I wanted her to have this woman and her world somewhere inside her—a woman who was a picture of independence and civility, who was funny and courageous and kind, and who carried a dose of the City's potion within her. I wanted my daughter to experience that. After that, Ann always asked about my daughter.

During those years, Ann would, from time to time, urge me to explore my Jewishness. I did not. But, because of her, I did look a fact about myself in the eye. I had my own dark secret. I am ashamed of being part Jewish—or *was* ashamed. And angry. I've always wanted to be *Christian,* that's what I feel I am, but my name won't let me. The name—Goodman—is there for all to see and hear and to associate with being Jewish. My name won't leave me alone. It's a very complicated subject, because my father was Jewish and my mother, dead now these ten years, was Christian. When they divorced, loyalties were challenged, and the differences between the two were made clearer. I think my father, dead only nine months now, was ashamed of being Jewish. I never saw him inside of a synagogue, except at his older brother's funeral. If *he* was ashamed, why shouldn't *I* be ashamed? Yet, part of me was so comfortable with the Jewishness I knew and loved in New York. All of these things Ann's words made me consider. It felt a safe subject with her. She was one of the least judgmental people I have ever met. That's why so many other people who knew her trusted her so. I could be myself with her. That was the gift she always gave me when I visited her.

I am still pondering this. I never would have faced up to it if it hadn't it been for Ann.

Then one day, some years later—I think Ann was eighty-three or so—during an ordinary visit, she said,
"Daniel came back into my life."
For a minute, I didn't know who she was talking about. Daniel. *Daniel!*
"He *did?* What do you mean, came back into your life?"
"He called."

"Oh my God. What did he say?"

"He said he missed me. That his wife had died. That if he was ever in New York, he'd like to see me."

"How did you feel about that?"

"I asked him why he'd never called me all these years. He didn't have an answer. I told him how much that had hurt me."

"And...?"

"And he said he was sorry. What else could he say?"

"So—will you see him?"

"I don't know. Maybe. It was nice that he'd been thinking of me all these years."

I saw in her that undeniable thing, love—or passion, obsession, whatever you want to call it. Even in the face of pain and humiliation, it can never be convinced of anything at all. It's headstrong, or heartstrong, and makes us follow its commands unquestioningly, like fanatics.

But she never did see Daniel again. He never came to New York. He called a few more times, I think. Then he gradually drew back into the shadows. It was an illusion.

Her dog, Gigi, grew old, as dogs do, and one day she wasn't there when I visited. Her death hit Ann hard. She looked wounded when I saw her. Then, when she was in her late eighties, Ann began to get sick—heart troubles. Eventually, she had to have a bypass operation. She'd had all the tests. It was unavoidable. So, she did. As with many old people, this set her back considerably. I had no idea how much until I visited her a month or so after her operation. She opened the door to her apartment in a robe. I almost gasped. She was another Ann.

The gauntness is what I remember most clearly. She had lost that robust, ample, cheery Ann forever. That Ann would never return. She looked changed, reduced, devitalized, as if the operation had sucked some of her life juices from her. Her face was the color of chalk. Her neck was stretched and had the instability of a baby chick. Wan and weak, she was. Where had my Ann gone?

She asked me in, moving carefully back to living room where she sat down. It had been a slow recovery, and would continue to be slow. It took great doses of spirit out of her. She was angry at the doctor for doing this to her. She felt it didn't have to be this way. She would have to go to the hospital every so often to get blood transfusions. Something had gone wrong. All those medical woes. They filled her appointment books now where lunches and concerts and visits used to.

"Look at me," she said. "Look at what they did to me."

"You'll bounce back. You always do."

"Yeah, right."

But it wasn't a "Yeah, right" of old. It was a bitter, sardonic "Yeah, right" that said, "I don't believe you, and you don't believe it yourself."

And no matter how much I wished it weren't so, she was in the great decline. She very seldom complained about her troubles. Sooner than I knew it, she was ninety. Her family in New York threw her a big party, and I went. It was at one of her niece's apartments on the Upper East Side, and the place was mobbed. Ann sat there, receiving, weak, but most pleased. It was a lovely moment for her to be honored for who she was. I saw the reach of her friendships then. I saw there were many others like me. Scores. Maybe hundreds.

It was when she turned ninety that she began to prepare to die. She had lived long enough, she said. She was never anything but lucid, but her body was not being kind to her and demanded more and more attention all the time. She wanted to die, but couldn't. She lived on still, and then she began to be frustrated and angry.

"I'm ready to go," she would say to me. "But I can't. I've lived my life. And now it's time for me to leave it."

Her insurance allowed her to have a nurse come and take care of her. She never had to leave her apartment, her home. I didn't see her for some months because of personal problems I was going through. Then one day I got a call from the nurse, a sweet woman from Barbados. She was direct,

"Ann is dying. If you want to see her before she goes, you had better come soon."

And I did. I came once more to that familiar apartment and entered. It had been converted to a nursing home in all but name. The place was shaded and quiet and smelled of medicine. Her own bed had been replaced by a hospital bed with guard rails and a gizmo for raising it and lowering it. The nurse sat in the semi-darkness next to the bed, ready to give Ann a shot or simply to minister. Ann lay there, breathing with difficulty, her eyes closed, and her mouth wide open in that characteristic near-death way of respiration. Oh, my Ann! My beautiful Ann!

I pulled up another chair next to the nurse.

"Can she hear me?" I asked.

"I think so. I told her you were coming. I think she understood."

I reached over and took Ann's hand. I held it lightly.

"Ann, sweetheart, it's Richard," I said. "It's Richard. I've come to see you."

I thought I heard a light moan of recognition, but I wasn't certain.

"I just wanted to say how much our friendship has meant to me. How wonderful you are."

I wasn't sure what else to say, and so I just held her hand for a while longer. The eminence of death was there, bitter and strong, and it was going to have its way. Ann had been in pain, the nurse told me, and she hoped she wouldn't have to suffer much longer.

Three days later, she died. I got a call from her niece, the one who had given her the birthday party, who told me the news.

Now, years later, I get on my bicycle and ride down that path next to the Hudson River to Greenwich Village. It's an exhilarating journey, and it always renews me. To peddle across Fourteenth Street, into the domain of the Village, is to enter another country. I always feel I've come home. I turn off from the path and bank down Charles Street into the heart of it all. When I pass by 302 West 12th Street, I look up to Ann's floor and think, I wonder if she's home. Sometimes, I even get off my bike and take two or three steps toward the building before I realize she's gone. I look up at her window. And I can her that voice, that quintessential New York voice, once again admonishing me, "You need to explore your...." Then, with her words echoing in my ear, I turn, sadly and gratefully, and walk away.

The Ceiling Leak

We had a lot of heavy rainstorms here in New York City this last summer. They were heavy even by New York standards, a place that will often shrug its shoulders at anything less than what might be signified world-class—a party, a sports contest, a skyscraper, a disaster. I heard the most violent rainstorm, which took place in late August, from my apartment in upper Manhattan, which began roughly at 4:30 AM. The thunderclaps woke me up.

"Thunderclaps" seems too meek a word for what entered my apartment. It was as if someone had snapped a gigantic sequoia in half. The thunder was so loud, you could practically visualize it, think of it as having mass, the sound occupied so much space in the air. There was lightening, too, of course, that preceded it, white spasms that jerked the air. Then the inevitable waiting for the thunder that came with so much brilliant noise. One thunderclap was so aggressively fierce I jumped in my seat. Afterwards, I looked down at my dog who seemed highly embarrassed by my fright.

Then came the rain. Ceaselessly. It's really no use for me to say how much it rained and for how long, because we all have our big rain stories. This is subjective stuff. I'll let the fact speak for itself: Most all the subways stopped running, and that is practically an unknown situation in New York City—the last time I recall it happening was after the 9/11 catastrophe. I can't think of a natural situation before that in thirty years of living here. Most of those that ceased functioning were simply flooded out of commission. This caused legions of problems that day, and the news was full of stories of the rain's havoc, and you heard them from friends and acquaintances all that day.

That's why when I woke up the following morning I wasn't especially surprised to see a darkish, bottle-shaped patch on my ceiling. It looked damp, and had that pre-drip hue to it—the ceiling not quite saturated yet, but almost. It went about halfway across my ceiling but wasn't that wide. It seemed, as these things go, fairly typical. The idea was, of course, to get the superintendent to come to fix it before actual water began dripping from the ceiling onto the floor, or, in this case, onto the bed, which is stationed partially underneath the patch.

The only curious thing is that I'm on the second floor, and there are four floors above me until you get to the roof where the rain had fallen so tumultuously. But I figured that the occupant in the apartment above me had done exactly what I'd done so many times—left her window open when she went away for the weekend or on vacation. The storm's strength being so severe and the quantity of rain so large, it had entered through the window and created a little flood in her apartment. If it could stop the subways, it could start a leak in my ceiling. I had experienced this sort of thing before, actually.

Then I noticed the smell.

It was a rank smell. At first I thought it might be garbage. Before the Noah-like rains we'd had, it had been unbearably hot in New York City for close to the entire week. And humid. Anyone who has spent a typical August in New York has often been confronted with the penetratingly pungent odor of roasting garbage, overripe in the ninety-plus degree noonday sun. It's an odor you don't soon forget and a kind of badge of honor for those with enough temerity to spend time in New York during that stygian month.

That's what the odor smelled like. Sort of. But not exactly. This odor really smelled like something you find in a crawl space, something that had once been alive and now is not. I thought perhaps the storm might have caused a squirrel or bird to have taken refuge from the noise and flash inside my open window and then had died in some obscure declivity of my room where an animal would go to die. I looked everywhere, under cabinets, behind drawers, in the closet. But I found nothing. The smell was putrid. The only way I can describe it with any sense of accuracy is to say that it was the smell of death.

That's when my eyes went to the patch on the ceiling. It was a little more glossy now, had a varnish-like sheen and was a bit sticky-looking, too. Then my curiosity got the better of me. If you can call it that. I got a chair and moved it under the stain. I stepped up on the chair for a closer look. My face was about a foot from the stain. It didn't seem to be water. It seemed to have a viscous texture. No, it wasn't water. I was about to touch it, to run my finger across its slick surface—I even considered tasting it—when I thought the better of it.

My heart sank at the realization. I knew for certain that this patch was the source of the foul smell.

After the police had come and forced opened the door of the apartment directly above me, they found the body. It was determined the lady—an older, rather stout woman with an impassive oval face who walked a small dog—had been dead for four days. In this heat. My dog, the one who wasn't scared of that extraordinary thunder, and who normally sleeps in the bedroom with me, refused to go in the bedroom. I should have suspected something. Dogs know the smell of death, and do not want to be in its presence. I didn't know the lady's name, and I only saw her infrequently.

Four days dead. Perhaps I should leave it to your imagination about what, exactly, that patch was on my ceiling. Perhaps not. Maybe some verbs might help. Suppurating. Fallen. Exploding. Decomposing. Putrefying. Then some nouns: Intestines. Effluvia. Liquids.

The body was removed by the morgue, but the police wouldn't let the superintendent in to clean the apartment until the woman's daughter came and emptied it of all personal effects first. So the rank smell—so relentless in its message of death—was still there. I was unable to sleep in my apartment that night. The odor of death: foul, ugly, pervasive, was ready to crawl under my skin. Since the stain on the ceiling remained, too, the idea that something might drip down from the apartment above was too horrifying even to contemplate. So I went to a friend's apartment to stay. Later that evening, I thought about what happened.

I didn't know the lady's name. She had a little dog, and I only saw her when our dog walking overlapped. She never looked at me when I passed by her. It wasn't so much that she averted her eyes as the fact that she looked past me, or through me, or around me.

She simply didn't see me. Or anyone else, I imagine. This seemed to be her way of avoiding dealing with the world, of evading contact. It preempted even a small exchange of "Hello" or "Good morning." This woman did not want to interact with the world. I didn't know her name, or she mine. I don't think I ever heard her speak. I never heard her voice.

The next few days I thought about what had happened. I realized that I hadn't come face to face with my own mortality. Who of us ever does? When someone dies, no matter how close to us, it's still a kind of abstraction. It's their death, not ours, and we go blithely on acting as if we were immortal. No, what I came face to face with is *how* I might die. I came face to face with this is the way we die sometimes, alone and rotting in our apartment for four days without anyone knowing we're dead. Four days, and no one noticed—not her daughter, who lives four blocks away—not anyone. It seemed unbearably sad.

I went out to walk my dog later that day, and when I returned I saw a woman, about my age, sitting on the stairs, weeping. A man was by her side with a tender hand on her shoulder and a consoling look. It was obviously the woman's daughter. Beside the woman was her mother's little dog. By this time, the coroner had arrived and the body had been taken away. I wondered if the daughter had been inside the apartment yet, had come face to face with the searing smell of death, of her mother's rotting, and even gone into the dreaded bedroom. I thought of saying something to her, but just looked at her understandingly and walked by her and up to my apartment.

The more I thought about it, though, the more I identified with the old lady. I thought: What is it about my decisions in life that have slowly but steadily left me alone? How have I lived that I've ended up like this? Solitary.

The woman's daughter, just minutes away, hadn't been to see her mother in at least four days—maybe more. I have a daughter, too, but she's only fourteen. She lives part of the time with her mother, part of the time with me. I ended the marriage six years ago, I think of that often. I think of the regrets I have about it. When people tell me they have no regrets, I know they're bloody liars. Everyone has regrets. It's just that some of us have more than others. Some of us make a career of producing regrets. I ask myself, how did I end up in this isolated situation? There are times when no one calls for days. This is partially to my satisfaction, but mostly it's not. I want company. I want interaction. Yet I do little to change things. Do people see me when I walk my dog the same way as they saw that poor old woman?

The fact is that some of us will die with friends and family at our side, holding our hand and speaking words of encouragement as we begin the last journey to wherever we must go. Some of us will have a priest or rabbi or minister near, comforting us with words we have heard all our lives in churches or in synagogues. Some of us will be reassured that God is waiting for us, and that we will be joining friends and loved ones when we pass on over to the other side. Others of us, though, will die alone, without a single person beside us, and rot in our beds, leaving a stinking smell as a reminder of our existence. I pray that someone is there with me, to hold my hand, and speak to me, as I die. Barring unforeseen circumstances, like a mortal accident or a sudden heart attack, this is to a great extent up to me, though. If I lead a solitary life, withdrawn and not engaged, and with few risks, and even fewer friends, what can I expect? This has haunted me in the days since. How I die will depend on how I live.

When I finally was able to return to my apartment three days later, my bedroom had been painted. The patch was gone. I wondered, though. Will, someday, the people in the apartment below me look up one morning and see me, or what's left of me, seeping through their ceiling? Will they smell my stink of death? Will I be that person about whom they'll ask themselves:

"Who was he? What was his name? He never said hello, he never spoke to us, he just walked his dog and didn't look at us as he passed by."

Appointment in Cortlandt

Last Saturday, I decided that I needed a healthy dose of nature. I live in Manhattan, and so I don't get a whole lot of wildness. I was missing the outdoors. I thought a day trip would be ideal, riding out on a train on one of the Metropolitan Transit Authority's lines, so I resolved to do just that. But where to go? I pulled out my trusty Hagstrom "50-Mile Radius From Columbus Circle New York City Map" to see what I could find in the way of inspiration. I wanted to go somewhere that was not too far (no more than ninety minutes) and not too close (no malls) where I could walk and hike—the woods, in other words.

My method? Very superficial and unscientific. I scanned my open Hagstrom. My eyes went northward, following the east side of the Hudson River, past Yonkers, Hastings-on-Hudson, Dobbs Ferry, Tarrytown, Croton-on-Hudson—and—what's this? I spotted a green, thumb-sized patch near Peekskill labeled "Blue Mountain Reserve." Or, to be precise, "Blue Mountain Reserv." Which, I suppose, could also mean "Blue Mountain Reservation"—or else someone was trying to save money by eliminating "e's." I'd never heard of it. It looked to be, as far as one can judge these things on a map, about five miles south of Peekskill, a town I'd never been to. I had accessed the MTA schedule on-line and saw there was a stop just before Peekskill, Cortlandt. I'd never heard of that, either. I reasoned that Cortlandt—which wasn't on my Hagstrom map, by the way (more about that later)—must be closer to the Blue Mountain Reserve than Peekskill.

I had my destination. Cortlandt.

I did a quick Google search—all of this was researched and decided within thirty minutes Saturday morning—for Blue Mountain Reserve, but I couldn't find much. (I did after I returned. My

Google skills must have been dull that morning.) What the hell, I concluded. The patch was green and fairly substantial. I decided to catch the 10:02 AM train at the 125th Street Station in Harlem. It was a pleasant day, brisk but not bitter. I put on my LL Bean light green lined jacket, packed a bird guide and notebook, and took off. I thought I might see some birds, even though the fall migration was all but over, but what I really wanted to see were the array of fall colors. I have a splendid view of trees across the Hudson on the Palisades from where I live, and lately they've been in high motley. I wanted more, wanted to be among them, up close and very personal.

So, off I went.

It's a wonderful view from atop the raised platform at the 125th Street Station in Harlem. You look *south,* toward Manhattan, to see a train approaching. Somehow, thinking of Manhattan as a *source* of trains seems slightly surreal. The train pulled in one minute late. The doors parted, I stepped in, and so began my little adventure. The train was only moderately full, and I had no trouble finding a seat by a window. Even though the MTA trains aren't true trains in the classic Santa Fe Special sense—they are smaller and more compact—I still felt the thrill of *travel by rail* surge through me. What is this atavistic pleasure that I feel when I get on a train? It seems more like an instinct, like some deep migratory urge, pulling at me, that makes me feel as if I *should* be doing this. What better form of travel is there? Especially nowadays. No one asks you to fasten your seatbelt, no one tells you to empty your change and other metal objects into a tray, no one demands you take off your belt or your shoes. The seats are generally wide enough for human accommodation. The world passes by you ever changing.

The train eased out of the station, and then slowly picked up speed. We crossed over into the Bronx and the train curled around, following the course of the Harlem River as it coursed toward the Hudson River.

The ride to Cortlandt would take just forty-eight minutes, so I sat back and enjoyed the view of the wide lovely Hudson. The tracks run right next to the river, and in fact so close sometimes you think you can reach down and touch the glossy water. I felt a spirit of adventure. It's funny how that spirit can overtake you, even if you know it's just a forty-eight-minute trip to a town in northern Westchester. It just simply *feels* like you're striking out for parts unknown, a sort of mini Amazon voyage, or trek to the Pole. Well, I hadn't ever been to Cortlandt, or to the Blue Mountain Reserve, had I? It was an adventure to me. I looked out at the wide Hudson River. It gets even wider as you travel north. It really *is* a beautiful river.

The train stopped at Yonkers, Tarrytown, Ossining—home of John Cheever! He who wrote the amazing *Falconer*. Was *this* the famous ancient prison right there by the river where Cheever had taught and that gave him the inspiration for his book? There was a structure. It looked forbidding. It had high walls with barbed wire on top. I couldn't be sure. What else could it be? I guess I had somehow pictured the prison in the country, near the woods. We sped on, stopped at Croton-on-Hudson, and then—Cortlandt.

I got off the train, along with three other people, and saw—a parking lot. That was it. Since it was Saturday, the parking lot was almost empty. The three people got into a car and sped off. I was left there alone. I probably should have taken this as a sign of some sort, but that would have been counterproductive. With the unknown, you should always expect the *unknown*. Where the hell was I? Was there an actual town of Cortlandt? Where was the Blue Mountain Reserv? I didn't see any signs of any kind. But I did see two MTA police cars parked next to one another in that classic this way/that way position allowing the drivers to talk to each other. I walked over. One of them saw me.

"Yeah?" the policeman said as I approached.

"Uh, I'm a serial killer...."

No, that's not what I said. But policemen always make me feel as if I should confess to something, even if I have to make it up.

I actually said, "I'm looking for the Blue Mountain Reserve."

"Yeah, it's around here. But you shoulda gotten off at Peekskill."

"Yeah, that's closer," the other officer said.

"There's a state police barracks down the road. I'd ask them," the first one said.

I thanked them and left. I walked down the empty road away from the train station—the road only went one way—and found the barracks. There was just one trooper there. I asked him how to find the Blue Mountain Reserve.

"That's easy. Take a left here at the light, walk about a half a mile until you come to Watch Hill Road, then turn left and just keep going."

All right, let's go! I walked out, turned left at the light and began walking. I found myself on the edge of one of those suburban-country roads that have two-inch shoulders at best. The cars whizzed by me ever so close. Zoom, zoom, zoom. A sidewalk? I didn't see a sidewalk the entire time I was there. One wonders if that's even in the town's vocabulary. I could picture a Ray Bradbury-like conversation with someone in Cortlandt.

"Do you have any sidewalks in Cortlandt?"

"Sidewalk? What is that? Leia, this man here speaks to us of 'side-walks'. Do you know what he means?"

"No, Zoran, I do not. Wait—many years ago I remember an uncle of mine—the one who imploded—who spoke to me of a 'side-walk.' I do not remember what he said they were. Are they dangerous?"

I walked along the edge of the road as SUVs and normal cars sped by me. Zoom! I walked by a small mall. So much for avoiding malls. A little later, I found Watch Hill Road and turned left as the trooper had instructed. I continued walking. I guessed I'd been walking for about thirty minutes and gone about two miles.

I wasn't sure exactly how far the Blue Mountain Reserve was, but it seemed to me it couldn't be that far, or else the state trooper would have mentioned that. Wouldn't he have? I was walking alongside a graytop road now with an even narrower shoulder than the first road. It was a shoulderette. I actually had to walk on the road itself from time to time, because the sides were a tangle of nonnegotiable thickets and boulders, and I simply could not walk there. The road wound around and up with quite a few blind turns. The SUVs—like so many anonymous hit men—plowed toward me and, catching sight of this *walker* at the last minute, swerved away just enough to avoid sending me to the Mayo Clinic. *Zoom,*

zoom, zoom. When you walk for a substantial distance on a suburban road with cars whizzing by you, missing you by two feet, or even one foot, you begin to fear for your life, and rightly so. I thought of all the writers who had been struck on the side of the road—Andre Dubus, Steven King, Randall Jarrell (well, Randall apparently jumped in front of the car). You also begin to question your sanity and your intelligence. *What am I doing here?*

What was I seeing? Well, not terribly much. I crossed a bridge and felt very Woody Guthrie. I walked by houses—not tract houses, but regular houses. I saw some trees. I kept going, risking my life, because I thought the Blue Mountain Reserve was just around the corner, or over the hill. A woman stopped her car at her mailbox, got out, retrieved the mail, and saw me. She quickly got back in her car, slammed the door and sped up her driveway. Who was I? An illegal alien? Or, worse, a *drifter?* I've always wanted to be a drifter—part-time, perhaps—because the word has a romantic, tidal allure to it, until so many serial killers ruined it by being drifters. I walked by a man mowing his lawn on the other side of the road. I had to find out where I was. I looked both ways and quickly crossed the road, narrowly missing being hit by an SUV. He stopped mowing when I approached. He looked around, as if to see what resources he had to protect himself, if necessary.

I asked him where was the Blue Mountain Reserve.

"You gotta go back to the blinking light there, and take a right and then go about three or four miles. There's some trails and stuff."

"Three or four *miles?*"

He nodded.

Three or four miles, and *then* the hiking would start. I'd already walked at least three miles. Now, three more. Then God knows how many miles of hiking. And then the walk back to the train station. I was already a nervous wreck from the cars nearly swiping me. I started to sing a version of my own Amy Winehouse song:

> They wanted to send me hiking
> But I said no, no, no.

I decided, reluctantly, to abandon my dreams of going to the woods. So, I turned back, more concerned than ever that I might be struck by a text-messaging, suburban SUV-driving, just-got-my-license-three-days-ago, I-hate-my-parents teenager. Looking over my shoulder every thirteen seconds, I finally reached the main road and started walking back to the train station. Then I began laughing maniacally. What an incredibly ridiculous day!

I saw a bus stop by the side of the road, glass enclosed, with some seats. I was fatigued. There was an older, red-haired woman seated there already. I took a seat next to her. She smiled. I was fairly certain, because of her age—she looked to be in her seventies—that her hair was not actually red. I heaved a sigh.

"How are you today?" I said to her.

"I'm fine, thank you. It's quite a nice day, isn't it?" That brogue of hers. I recognized it.

"It certainly is. There aren't many sidewalks around here, are there?"

"No!" she said with great emphasis. Her eyes widened.

"You're not from Cortlandt, are you?"

"No. Forest Hills, Queens," she said smiling. "And I miss it *terribly*."

"So is this retirement here for you?"

"Well, sort of. A few years ago I had a stroke, and my son, who was living here at the time, begged me to sell my house and come up here and live near him. But last year, he moved to Florida!"

"Oh, no. Left you high and dry?"

"Now I can't afford to move back. It's too expensive. But in Queens, I used to be able to walk everywhere. Oh, there were busses, but I always walked. I loved it!"

"Yeah, and they do have sidewalks in Queens."

"Everywhere!"

I started yearning for my sidewalks of New York, and for the ability anyone there has of walking everywhere for mile and miles. I wished I were there, that very moment, walking. Walking on a sidewalk, without fear of being struck dead by an SUV.

"I don't think they have many sidewalks in Cortlandt," I said.

"Not many."

"Say, where *is* Cortlandt—the town?" I asked her.
"There is no town."
"What?"
"This whole area is called Cortlandt. It includes towns like Croton."
"But the train station. It says 'Cortlandt.'"
"Oh, that's only five years old."
"No wonder I'd never heard of it." I took a deep breath. "So Cortlandt doesn't actually exist?"
"No."
"What about the Blue Mountain Reserve."
"I don't think I've ever heard of that."

Take the "A" Train

What am I doing on New York City's "A" train at eleven o'clock on a Tuesday night, once again making the hour-long journey back from her place to mine at my age? Which is sixty. I feel homeless, disheveled, half-asleep, depleted, and grungy. I'm well on my way to having to shave. I've gotten undressed at her place, and dressed again, and soon I'll get undressed at my place again. With so much undressing and dressing, I feel like a runway model—if a runway model could weigh 180 pounds, have a thirty-five-inch waist and a receding hairline. She gave me a great dinner, as she always does. She's a fantastic cook, superb, really. She has the touch, the skill. She knows food, understands it, and eating her dinners is sublime.

God knows, I can stand a good meal. I manage to do well enough by my fourteen year-old daughter when she stays with me. But the kitchen in my apartment is small, nearly as small as the kitchen of my first New York apartment thirty years ago—or maybe it's smaller. Yes, it's smaller. When I was in my twenties during those early Manhattan years, cooking in a small kitchen was an adventure, and I rose to the challenge. I didn't mind the half-oven above the burners, or the gymnast-like maneuvers I had to make to reach a pot if there were two of us in the kitchen. I remember making meals my girlfriend loved and that guests loved: cassoulet, soul food from my Virginia roots, *coq au vin,* and the *tarte au pomme* I learned to make at a French restaurant in Cambridge where I'd worked once thirty years ago.

But the kitchen I now possess at age sixty I do not consider an adventure. I just consider it small. So, when my daughter is not here, I tend not to cook much of anything. I'm not at the Dinty Moore stew stage yet, but I'm probably closer than I would like to think. This is one reason why I love eating at her place in Tribeca. Oh, the things she makes! The most unusual and scintillating soups, for example.

"What's that taste?" I ask her, my mouth loving it, but curious. This is a cold, complex soup.

"Guess," she says.

"Hmm. Difficult."

It's a purée, so no help from the texture. All vegetables, I'm pretty sure. Color: some subtle, pale hue of green. It's more than three ingredients, I suspect.

"Parsley?"

"No. Guess again."

I thought I was pretty good at this.

"I...can't. I give up."

"Watercress."

"Oh—brilliant!" I find it there on my tongue: watercress, of course.

She has some artisan bread and a fine white wine, cool, and exuding character. Her table is long and wooden, and she has several candles that flicker in the summer twilight. It's simple, and it's grand. We're eating in her small but light-filled apartment in Tribeca, one of the neighborhoods of New York I love the most. It's an old part of the city, with massive brick warehouses upon which light plays in so many delicious ways. And there are still cobblestoned streets! You feel the human hand in this neighborhood. One of her walls is covered in books, mostly art books, because she works as an art critic for a very good magazine. She's about my age, from another country, has been here for years, speaks idiomatic English at this point, but still has the hauteur of being European. There is a sense she gives off that Europeans are better than Americans. I don't try to dissuade her of that notion, since it obviously helps to sustain her, like being born in Connecticut still sustains some Americans.

She's a very lively, funny, smart woman. I feel lucky to have found her. Yes, it was on the Internet. We bantered back and forth and finally arranged to meet. That first time was a Saturday afternoon, and it happened to be raining furiously. We had arranged to meet at a café—the classic neutral place all girlfriends of the prospective bride say to meet the future groom. I called her from under an awning nearby. I was getting drenched by the downpour, so she asked me up. Later, she would say that her girlfriends told her she was crazy to let a strange man into her apartment.

"You don't look like an ax murderer," she says cheerily as I walk in.

"No, I'm not," I say, as if I have to respond to this. I feel too old to be an ax murderer. The ax would be too heavy for me. Why is it that women who meet you for the first time are always concerned you might be an ax murderer? Isn't there anything else you might be? I suppose being an embezzler, or an arsonist would be just fine.

I sit down in a chair opposite her, somewhat rigid, as if I were meeting a parent for the first time. My shirt is clinging to my shoulders from the rain. She says I don't look like my photo, and I tell her neither does she. She has a bottle of white wine, a Pouilly-Fuissé, and though it is only three o'clock, we start in on it. The rain pours, and we drink the cool wine from France with the medieval lettering on the label and get to know one another. Once again, she brings up the ax:

"So, I guess you really aren't an ax murderer. You have your own website. And you've published some things. So I feel safe."

Haven't criminals published?

I ask her, "You're not an ax murderer either, are you?" I don't want her to feel left out.

She laughs. It's a very good thing to make a woman laugh.

It isn't long before the Pouilly-Fuissé enters the equation, and she asks me to sit next to her. Not too long afterward, we are kissing. Oh, it's been so long since I've kissed a woman. I touch her hair, glide my fingers through the lushness of it. Then, well, soon after, I find her pliant nipple in my mouth, and I think the afternoon is going rather well.

"Do you think we're going to have an affair?" she asks me.

"Uh," I answer, thrown by my own unuttered thoughts being read.

I finally leave before consummation, because I am fairly bombed, and it doesn't seem right. Later I wonder if this was just an idiotic stance of mine. So begins the first in a series of long subway rides back to my apartment, which is at the polar opposite end of Manhattan, in states of being that were often hazy at best. It is always at her place where we meet, because her place is more interesting and fun and because she makes these gorgeous meals. Since she works at a demanding job, the earliest we can meet during the week is seven in the evening. By the time we talk, and she cooks, and we eat, and everything else, it is after eleven o'clock when I leave. This is how I find myself so often on the subway in an altered state—sort of 75 percent me, or maybe even 65 percent me. At that hour, the subway doesn't come right away, so I stand there amongst the other eleven-plus PM characters on the platform, and think.

There is nothing like standing on a sparsely populated subway platform late at night waiting to go home when you're sixty to make you wonder if your life is going in the right direction. Why am I doing this? I am doing this because I want some affection, and touch, and company. I want some intimacy. Age doesn't matter when it comes to that, does it? We need it from the day we're born until the day we die. I think we need it more when we're older, actually. I knew a woman who once said to me, "It's not good to go even one day without being touched." How about one year? *That's* not good. Of course, I sometimes have a hard time distinguishing between intimacy and lust, but that's another issue. I do know that at the very least I want to kiss her and to be kissed by her, because kissing was and always will be one of the most intimate, revealing and exciting forms of communication between a man and a woman. And there we are, man and woman.

The women I meet at this stage of my life eventually want to know what went wrong with my marriage. I was married for nine years, and my wife and I had a child. Then we divorced. This woman is no different; she wants to know what went wrong with my marriage. She was married very briefly when she was young. I'd rather talk about almost anything else. I feel protective toward that relationship. Two people tried to make it work, one not hard enough—that would be me—and it didn't. Sometimes I wish I could answer these inquiring minds by saying, "She left me for another man."

Or, even better, "She left me for another woman." Or, "She wanted to have children. I didn't." But that wouldn't be true.

After we decided to divorce—my idea, of course—there came a day before I moved out that the formal papers arrived. I had to sign them, and that would be that. I knew they were coming. There had been no turning back for a long while. My wife—so soon to be ex-wife—handed them to me. I looked them over perfunctorily. Then I suddenly felt so downcast. I felt unbearably sad. I was so disappointed in myself. It all went back to those vows I made standing next to her nine years earlier. I'd heard them spoken hundreds of times before at weddings and in movies and in books. "For better or worse...in sickness and in health...." Here I was, unable to keep them. When I made those vows they were far more important than I ever could know, and here I was, unable to keep them. I had not been a good husband, and this, I knew, as I shakily signed the paper, was one of the four or five things that are unequivocally important in life. Something that has nothing to do with talent or money or social standing, but with character, compassion, and courage. Real tests of who you are at your very core.

Some summer evenings in the glory of twilight she and I go to the rooftop, where there is a table and chairs and many high-growing plants in russet Italian terracotta containers. We bring up the gorgeous food she's made and sit and dine and look out onto lower Manhattan and talk. What a sense of promise this view of Manhattan gives! You feel as if you could make a life here, make some sort of difference. We talk mostly about her.

"I feel European," she says, bringing this up yet again. "There is some part of me that will always be European, no matter how long I've been in America."

She means of course that she will always have an understanding of culture that is more profound, *truer*, than I will ever have. Part of me believes this, while another part of me feels she's behaving like someone who has inherited her wealth, with a lofty, hollow sense of assumption. She inherited Europe. She didn't earn it. Even if I know far more about certain aspects of that culture, though, it doesn't matter. I'm only a naturalized citizen.

She has virtually no curiosity about my writing. This, more than anything, is the slight that galls.

Honestly? I love sleeping with her. I love being with her, because she's smart, she's learned, she loves books and has read widely and hungrily, she loves music, she's a hard worker, and she's made her way in the world all by herself. When I leave her apartment in the evening for the walk to the subway, she stands behind the door naked, sometimes leaning out slightly in the vacant hallway to throw me a kiss.

Still, I have an old yearning. One day I tell her that while I don't know where this is going, I'm looking for a committed relationship—yes, marriage, if it comes to that. What about her?

"No, I have no desire to get married."

"What do you want?"

"I want to have fun. I want to be simulated. I don't want anything heavy."

She wants a man *around* her life. She admits as much, eventually, when I press her on it. "Yes, you're right," she says. "I like my life the way it is. I worked hard to get here. I'm happy, mostly."

She asks me to come out to her weekend house in—yes—Connecticut many times, and each time I find a reason not to. Why is this? She'll cook for me, and we'll sit on the wide porch she's described to me so often, and look out to a low-slung valley where the mist crawls across hauntingly. We'll drink more of her brook-cold Pouilly-Fuissé. And we'll make love. And kiss. So, why do I always find a way to dodge her invitations? Do I know these visits will lead to nothing more than an affair, albeit one that replenishes and excites and simulates me? Or is there something else? Some deeper, well-hidden fissure of mine? Well, most likely, since I never stay over at her place. She asks me, but I tell her that I have a dog, and he needs walking, and so I have to leave. Of course, I could make arrangements for that if I wanted to.

Sometimes on the subway going down to her place I'll see a family together. It's odd, but you seldom see local families on the subway in New York City—I mean the whole unit—except returning from a baseball or basketball game, from the beach or from the circus. But you do see tourist families. They have the classic American look, with dad and mom and sis and brother in bright new jeans or shorts and one of them checking out a guidebook intently or a subway map. When I look at them, I have to strongly disagree with Count Tolstoy. All happy families are *not* alike. Each is different in its own way.

When I look at these families, I yearn for what they have, and for what I abandoned. I don't want to romanticize it, and I won't. I know how hard it is to maintain a family. I also know how much it can provide. I do now, anyway. A good working family is a place where everyone can be themselves. It's a place where what you do as an individual matters. It doesn't matter in so much of the world, or in a bad family. In a good family, though, a working family, they care about *you*. No one will ever give you, the individual, as much care and attention.

I hear people who are divorced talk all the time about their decision. Most of them say the same thing in so many words, especially if they have children: It was a hard decision, but I was so miserable that I couldn't function. I couldn't love my kids the way they needed to be loved. My partner and I were fighting all time. It was terrible. I knew I'd be a better parent if I got out of the marriage. I'd be happier with myself.

Well, I'm looking at this from the perspective of having left my marriage six years ago, so the element of regret is far stronger now than the despair I was feeling at the time. Now I see all too clearly, on the subway, in the faces of those families. I see what I bartered for my so-called freedom. I gave away a working unit that could withstand almost anything, even life's worst blows, and where I felt safe, and strong, and needed, and appreciated. Where every day, if people were doing their job, we all did something to make the unit tougher, more resilient, more capable. It's such a simple idea, the family. It's also ancient, it runs as far back in time as our recorded history, and it has endured for a reason. We who ignore that emotional tensile strength do so not only at our peril, but with a sense of haughtiness, as if we were ignoring the wisdom of the ages.

If this sounds like something you might hear in a church in rural Georgia, I don't care. It's what I've learned.

It astounds me that the woman I go to visit on the subway doesn't want this, doesn't want a family, or at least being a couple. She doesn't, though. She doesn't want to give up her independence. Or, really, her supremacy. Because in a family, if it's functioning halfway right, no one is supreme. The family is. She knows that, and I'm sure the contemplation of losing her supremacy makes her queasy. But that's her choice. I'm sad, because it's so much fun being with her. She is taking her own subway ride, too, from work to her apartment where she lives alone—except for visits from someone like me. That's what she wants. We are literally two trains passing in the night.

The truth is, though, as long as we're trying hard to tell the truth here, that I'm relieved. I'm grateful that she doesn't want something more serious. I've had a bellyful of failure. I look in the mirror, and sometimes I don't like what I see. What is it I want? So many women have asked me this.

Then comes that period of lame duck romance where both of us know the future is doomed, and that it will lead to nothing, at least in terms of us. I'm still going to see her. But inevitably, there will come a day when I'm no longer standing on the subway platform late at night after a splendid meal and a kiss goodnight as she stands nude just behind her partially opened door. I will take the "A" train, one final time, with all the other late night souls, home.

The Wheaton Girl

I'm looking at some photographs of her when she was a student at Wheaton College in the late 1930s. In one of them she's in a riding outfit—jodhpurs, with helmet, riding boots, crop, and a white ascot—that makes me think of Ginger Rogers in *Top Hat*. In terms of beauty, she could give Ginger a run for her money. She was just as handsome in that wonderful *American* way. She was wholesome, sporty, with a bright optimism about her so many American women have—or had. She looks so at home outdoors. In another photo, she's sitting on the ground holding a pair of ice skates and wearing the puffiest white gloves you've ever seen and a hunter's cap. I can see why my father fell in love with her. She's vibrant—girlish and womanly at the same time, and such optimistic eyes. She looks so full of life. Topsy—Marianna—Mother.

She met my father, Dick Goodman, while she was at Wheaton. He was at Yale. He'd grown up in Norfolk, Virginia, she in Dayton, Ohio. She was introduced to him by her roommate, Elsa, whose boyfriend was my father's fraternity brother. How long was it before they fell in love? Weeks? Months? I wish I could have talked to her back then, could have known her in her glory days. I would like to have talked to her before she met my father, before love and marriage took over her thoughts. What did she like to discuss? What was her sense of humor like as a very young woman? Did she tell jokes? Make quips? What causes was she passionate about? What books did she love? What music?

"They were the best times of my life," she said of those years at Wheaton. It was an all-girls school back then, in a small town in southeastern Massachusetts, between Boston and Providence. She adored Wheaton, adored learning, adored her friends, and the place itself. I can't help but think what it was like for her, a young Dayton girl, coming east on the train to begin her freshman year. Everything about the great college experience was in the East, and here she was, going to see, and to have, it all herself.

She got the nickname "Topsy" at college. This is the name I knew her as when I was a boy, though I never called her that. How did she get it, I asked her once.

"Well, Elsa said, 'We can't call you Marianna. It's too dull. You need another name. Let's see, Flopsy, Mopsy, Topsy—or Cottontail.' I told her it wasn't going to be Flopsy, Mopsy or Cottontail, so it would have to be Topsy."

So, everyone called her Topsy, including my father. I didn't know her real name was Marianna until I was older. Later in her life, after things had gone bad, she began calling herself Marianna again. Gradually, Topsy, along with so much else in her past, dropped away.

After my mother died, I found some old albums and notebooks of hers in her room in Florida. One of them is a scrapbook of her years at Wheaton. It's so typical of that time, jam-packed with memorabilia of a girl at college in the 1930s. It's fat with invitations to dances and to teas; pasted with tickets to football games at Harvard, Yale and Dartmouth; with matchbooks from the Stork Club and the Waldorf Astoria pasted in; with tickets to Broadway plays (*Idiot's Delight*, starring Alfred Lunt and Lynne Fontanne); with telegrams, so many telegrams! What a lovely way to communicate! Even the most ordinary message somehow manages to be urgent, yet personal, in that staccato print: "Will be at the Ritz Carlton this weekend Can you come visit Would adore to see you Elise"

Her scrapbook is such a jazzy book. It's the record of a young woman having a splendid time in that bygone era. When I turn its pages, so crammed with festivity, I feel like F. Scott Fitzgerald is looking over my shoulder. In the Class Will of her 1940 yearbook, the year she graduated, it says, "Topsy Rehling leaves Wilbur, the raccoon coat to Pat Kuehner." A raccoon coat!

The man she met through her roommate was a beautiful young man, slender, graceful and charming. Oh, how my father would be disgusted by my calling him "beautiful"! But I have seen photographs of him at Yale, and if you saw them, you would say so, too. In one of them, he's wearing tennis shorts and a T-shirt, and a tweed sports jacket, so much the style back then. He's lying on the grass, on his side, and his slim legs are graceful, slightly bent, in that languid way that is almost feminine. He has curly hair and an easy smile. Although he seldom talked to me about his life, I know he was on the boxing team and the lacrosse team, though he didn't have much time for sports or recreation. So, he would have been athletic. He would have been fit. He was a scholarship student. This was the Depression, and his father, who was in real estate, had lost most everything. He told me he washed dishes in the school cafeteria to earn spending money.

I wish I could transport myself back in time to listen to the early conversations between Topsy and Dick. I wonder if she made *him* laugh. In the later years of her life, laughter was everything to her. She searched for it like a parched man searches for water in the desert. I wonder, too, if my father was jealous of her intelligence, of her mind. Years later, she told me that she had a large collection of classical records. "After we were married, he made me throw them all away," she said. That, probably more than anything else she said about him, shocked me the most.

I'd like to have been there while they walked together on the Yale campus, when they went to a football game on a sharp fall day. When they went to dinner at some local dive. Did they go to New York City together? I knew my father went down to New York from Yale. Did he take my mother with him? The mighty Empire State Building had been completed just a few years earlier. Did they go to the top? Were those matches from the Stork Club in her yearbook from an evening with him? Sometimes when I walk the streets of New York where I live—especially the nocturnal New York I know existed back when they were young—I think of them and wonder if I'm walking where they might have walked. I've eaten in a restaurant in Little Italy I know my father went to when he was at Yale. On a visit once to New York to see me, he pointed it out as we walked. "It's still there," he said with a smile of remembering.

I tried to put myself back in time when I went to Yale for the first time a few years ago to teach a course in writing and to give a reading. All these years of living in New York, and I'd never been to New Haven. My host walked me around the campus and through the old stone buildings. Though I'd never stepped inside those buildings before, I had the sense of being in the presence of ghosts. I knew my father had been in some of them, and probably often, as a young man. I knew, too, that he must have walked with Topsy across the Yale campus. Perhaps they had played tennis together one afternoon. Perhaps she had taken this photo of him lying on the grass in his tweed jacket and shorts. I was filled with a sense of nostalgia for something that I never experienced.

She fell in love with my father. There was never any doubt. She never once disavowed that, no matter how bitter the times later. "I was so in love with your father," she said to me more than once. Take care of her, Daddy, I want to plead with him across time. She's so beautiful, and smart, and generous. Protect her. Love her. He doesn't listen, though.

After she graduated from Wheaton, my mother came back to Dayton, to the town where she grew up. She was a Midwesterner through and through, "down to my very bones," as she used to say. I didn't know that when I was a boy. Or I didn't understand what that meant. To me, since I grew up in Virginia, my mother must have grown up there, too. Such is the ego of a child. I went to Dayton a few times when I was a boy, but I was too involved with my own boyhood to think about her childhood. Her parents, George and Edna, lived in a big Tudor-style home on a hill with a long, winding driveway. She had a younger sister, Dottie, but Topsy was the more brilliant, the more beautiful—like Ginger Rogers, only she didn't have to have her dialogue written for her.

Back home after Wheaton, Topsy went to work for the *Dayton Daily News*. This was something else I didn't know when I was a boy. I asked her about this much later.

"I worked for the *Dayton Daily News* from 1940-43," she wrote to me from Florida toward the end of her life, "on what they called the society page. It was just that—engagements, weddings, etc., and a gossip column re the comings and goings of Dayton society.

After I was there about a year, I started writing a Sunday column called "And Incidentally..." about the younger 'elite' and events pertaining to them. Don't you love it? Society in Dayton! And believe me they took it seriously. A lot of men were off to the wars so I got assignments I wouldn't have ordinarily. I reviewed all the movies and plays. Live theatre was pretty good. Wright-Patterson field was nearby so entertainers came there.

"As I look back, I guess this was the happiest time of my life. Oh—maybe the Wheaton days were the best."

I called the *Dayton Daily News*, and they sent me some copies of my mother's column. I don't know what I expected. But here's part of a typical column from December in 1941. She was twenty-four.

And Incidentally...
by Marianna

Party week, and no rest for the weary bones! But who cares—'tis time to make merry, and Christmas comes but once a year. Homes are studded with shining jewels of reds and greens and blues that are only unearthed from the household safety deposit box this once during the year. And New Year's is just around the corner...A party, or a wedding, or a dance—it's something every day, and every minute is bulging with things to do.

And speaking of parties, one of the best yet was Frances Kennedy's debut Monday night at the Country club. In the wee small hours, the dancing, wining and dining was still in full swing in the midst of green profusion.

Dancing around in good looking gowns were Fredericka Patterson and Shirley Kirkpatrick, 'mongst a bevy of other good-looking gals.

Fredericka was wearing a champaign gold net dress with gold lame trim, and Shirley's dress had a silver lame bodice with a black net skirt with yards and yards. A clever idea was hers—she wore a black net mantilla caught with a silver bow in her hair.

The date of this column? December 28, 1941, just three Sundays after the Japanese attack on Pearl Harbor. Where is the War in all this?

To me, what is so wonderful about this isn't the writing—how else could you write about those things back then?—but the fact that she did it. Right out of college, and she had her own newspaper column. Meanwhile, she was engaged to my father. Star-crossed lovers who would divorce later. Once, prowling through her scrapbooks, I found a photograph of her in a local newspaper. She's gorgeous, in a long chiffon black and white gown. She looks both enticingly languid and virginal in that way only engagement photos of long ago could make a young woman look. I thought—how lucky to discover the photo of her engagement to my father. The caption read: "Mr. and Mrs. George H. Rehling, of 'Beverwyck,' on Ridgeway Road, are announcing the engagement of their daughter to Capt H. Franklin Maurer, Jr." *Franklin Maurer?* I read the text again. Later, there must, of course, have been a broken engagement to this Franklin Maurer. What happened? There is no date on this clipping, but it does go on to say that she had graduated from Wheaton, so it must have been after 1940 and during the time she worked for the *Dayton Daily New*s. Years later, when she was bitter and hopeless, she once spat out, "I should have married Frank Maurer!" She didn't, though.

"Thanks, Mom," I said.

Instead, she married my father in Dayton at her home. They moved to Virginia Beach, Virginia. My father had grown up in Norfolk, and his parents had a summer house in Virginia Beach. This is where Topsy and Dick went to live. A fatal mistake, I am sure. She gave up the newspaper column and job. This was still a time when a woman dropped everything—her own family, her job, her friends, her name—to be with her husband, wherever that was. Much later, after we had moved away, after Michigan, she talked to me about moving into that big house and my father:

"If only he'd gotten just a little apartment. Something we could have called our own. I wouldn't have cared if it wasn't grand. I didn't need all that room in that big house."

She was talking about the house at 107 63rd Street where I grew up. This is where my father took his bride to live and to raise a family. His own father would only live a few years more, but his mother, my grandmother, came and lived with us for four months every summer as long as they were married. I loved that house, but it was not my mother's house. She never had a house of her own. My father could have afforded a little place, even at the start. His business—building supplies—did reasonably well. You have to have something of your own together when you start, if you possibly can. You have to build your own life. My father chose not to do that. Was he ashamed to start out so meagerly? It looks that way. It looks like he was afraid to be young and married and in love. Shame, I think, guided him all too well.

That trip south nearly seventy years ago: my mother entered a lush, sandy, breezy, hot southeastern Virginia community. In the summer, Virginia Beach swelled like a sponge to three times its size with tourists and itinerants. After Labor Day, it shrunk to its fall, winter and spring size. Topsy stepped into a Southern world, specifically a Virginia world, and even more specifically a Tidewater world, that had a strict culture all its own. She stepped into a world in which black people played a more prominent role than she'd ever experienced. The end of the Civil War was a mere eighty years before. Consider that today the end of the Second World War is just sixty years ago, and we still feel its human echoes. It's not that she'd never seen a black person before, or talked to one. It's just that she'd never encountered the Southern way of accommodating blacks. This was a part of the country in which slavery had flourished. Segregation was real. It was the law. You do not erase the way a people's mindset simply by laws. My father and grandmother and the people of that time and that place looked upon black people—colored people, as they called them—as servants.

She also learned that my father had a secret. Or at least I think it was a secret. This part of the story is murky, a bit hard to sort out. My father was Jewish. From all I can tell, he was ashamed of that. He tried to hide it. I don't see how you can hide at least a suspicion that you might be Jewish with the last name of Goodman. My mother claims she didn't know he was Jewish until they went to Virginia. This was on a trip before they were married.

"I didn't know he was Jewish for three or four years," she said. She meant when she was at Wheaton, and he was at Yale.

"How did you find out?" I asked her.

"We drove down to Virginia Beach. He would point to a house and say, 'That's where my cousin lives.' The name was Hofheimer. Then he'd point to another and say, 'That's where my friend lives...' and give another Jewish name. This was his way of telling me he was Jewish. I was surprised he'd hidden it."

She thought this was one of the guiding motivations of his life. "Everything he did," she said, "was geared toward hiding being Jewish." Though I was raised Christian by my mother, for years I denied that half of me is Jewish. I inherited that shame from my father. It's different now—at least I think so.

The oppressive heat! I grew up in it, and am used to it, and even am drawn to it, but Topsy was not. She hated it. How it must have weighted her down. At least her house was near the ocean. At least she had those sea breezes every so often. The heat was nothing compared to the characters that entered her life, though. She made some good friends in Virginia Beach, some who were loyal and kind. But she had two formidable adversaries—my grandmother, and my aunt. Both disliked her and were jealous of her for different reasons. My grandmother—my father's mother—worshipped my father, and no woman would ever be good enough for him. My aunt, married to my father's older brother, was not only jealous, but spiteful. She and my uncle lived in Virginia Beach as well, so they saw a lot of my father and my mother.

So here arrived this beautiful Northern girl, college educated, Episcopalian, from Dayton, Ohio, well spoken, well read, kind, and in love—and she *was* so deeply in love with my father—into my aunt's world. Topsy was everything my aunt was not, and never would be. Even if you discount the religious aspect of it all—my aunt was Jewish—there remained the element of my mother's character and heart and beauty, none of which my aunt had, or ever would. She did have guile and cunning and a smoldering desire to hurt my mother, though. And she did. I am not suggesting that my aunt or my grandmother—even taken together—were responsible for my mother's undoing, or for the fact that she started drinking. But they weren't a consolation, either.

Even after the divorce, after Topsy had lived in Michigan for years—even after she moved to New York City—my aunt was still capable of striking her, like a viper. I remember coming to my mother's apartment in New York one day some years ago and talking about Virginia. Somehow we got onto my aunt. By then, my father had remarried a much younger woman. When he and his new wife had a little baby girl, my aunt called my mother in New York.

"And do you know what she said to me?" my mother told me, her voice beginning to crack. "She said, 'Oh, Topsy, you should *see* this baby. She's *so* beautiful! *So* darling!'" My mother began to cry, the tears streaming down her cheeks, the agony on her face. "Can you imagine—calling *me* and saying, 'The baby is *so*…beautiful?'" My mother, who still, and always, loved my father, heard this from my aunt, about the child of my father's second, much younger and very beautiful wife. I remember, too, not terribly long ago, sitting in my uncle and aunt's house in Virginia Beach and that same aunt saying to me, "It must have been hard for you growing up, what with your mother *drunk* all the time." She placed dramatic emphasis on the word *drunk,* like she was hitting me with it. And I did feel it. I remember my aunt looked at me after she said it, with that look all bullies have after they've said or done something cruel, waiting to see, and to savor, the pain. This is what my mother faced on an almost daily basis.

"I thought it was going to be different," my mother said to me once. "I can tell you that. I didn't know there was going to be such an overwhelming Goodman influence. I had to submerge myself in their presence."

But now I want you to know how much I loved her as a child, and how beautiful and capable she was. Because that is as important to this story as her decline and fall, and I want you to see the best in her. She can't speak for herself anymore. It's up to those who knew her to protect her. When we no longer talk about someone, when we no longer conjure their beauty and the good things they did—their laughter, the way they walked, held their fork, brushed their hand through their hair, the way they drove a car, sat and read a book, argued with us, cried tears, and slept—then we are co-conspirators in their vanishing.

I loved having her as my mother, and I knew nothing of what was going on in her adult life with my father, or with anyone else. Later, that would change, but when I was young, she was a large lovely presence I would follow about the house. She had soft brown hair, fair skin, an easy smile and wore brilliant red lipstick. She had pretty legs and arms, and her jewelry tinkled when she walked about. When she was happy, she whistled. Whistled! Merry tunes, sweetly whistled. Oh, yes, I was in love with her! Deeply, madly. I've tried to liberate myself from her, but I'm still tied to her. Even now.

   I remember when she would come upstairs to kiss me goodnight. I waited for that with so much longing. This was the most exquisite moment of the day for me. To see and feel her bending over me, that beautiful figure, and to have her lovely face so close to mine, and to hear her say to me, "Good night, Sweetie," and then to give me a kiss—this was the moment I waited for. I could smell her perfume and feel her presence so strongly. She was the most beautiful woman on earth, and for a moment—a brief moment—she was mine. I wanted her to stay. "Don't go, Mommy!" I said. But she went. "Now go to sleep," she said. "The sandman is coming soon. He's bringing you sweet dreams." I wanted the sandman, but I wanted her more. "One more kiss, Mommy! Please!" Sometimes she would say yes, and I would be overjoyed at my luck—to have two goodnight kisses from her. But she did leave, after all, and I was left with the sound of her soft words in my ear, the pretty noise of her rustling dress, and the scent of her perfume in the air. Many years later, when I read the passage at the beginning of *Remembrance of Things Past,* when the boy Marcel waits so desperately for his mother to come to kiss him goodnight, my mind and heart flew back to those nights in Virginia when I waited with such anticipation, too.

   When I was a boy, Topsy stayed home with us. There were three of us, my brother and sister, who were twins, who were just twelve months younger than I. Three children within twelve months. She said once to me, "I was outside in the back yard with you kids when you were very young one day and I couldn't find Mary." Mary was my sister. "I panicked. I looked everywhere!" Pause. "Mary was on my knee." I was jealous of the twins, and the attention they received from my mother, but there was nothing I could do.

   "You were not a cuddly baby," my mother said to me years later. "Something happened. You withdrew—because of the twins."

Yes, I know. I'm still trying to reappear.

Our days in Virginia Beach, especially in the summer, were filled with the scents and sounds of outdoors, of gardenias, of honeysuckle, of the briny smell of the ocean which was just a few hundred yards away—all of them aroused by the searing heat of the long Virginia summer day. We had gardenia bushes in our front yard, and in the summer, the smell of gardenias went straight into my body like morphine. I was almost naked, in my bathing trunks all day. I ran through the entire Virginia summer day like that. The scents and smells of the hot day, the heated grass, and the ocean-infused air awakened me. Every sensation stroked my body—the scent of figs, the ebb and flow of ocean smells, and the scent of gardenias. I breathed summer.

In the evening, my mother would sometimes clip three or four gardenias from a bush. The smells of summer quietly settled down to their evening lives. My mother would put the gardenias in a boat-shaped silver bowl full of cool water. I watched the water bead and slide on the side of the cold bowl. She placed the bowl in the center of the dinner table. The gardenias floated on the cool water's surface. As we ate our supper, I would from time to time look at the floating gardenias. Nothing in the world was as white. White floating gardenias. Sometimes my mother would put a gardenia in her hair. She would place the flower into her brown hair, which was thick and full. She then became transformed into a kind of mermaid on land. I couldn't keep my eyes off her. I couldn't, even if she was just placing forks and knives on the table.

In the summer, we went to the beach twice a day, which was only a few hundred yards away. I could see its azureness from my bedroom window on the second floor. My mother hauled us and all the heavy beach paraphernalia down from our house to the ocean where we swam and played in high joy for two or so hours while she sat either alone or with other mothers and talked, never fully relaxed as her eye would dart toward the water to make sure we were accounted for.

We had a big wide porch, and sometimes my parents would have people over in the early summer evening for drinks. The men would arrive from work in their seersucker suits, and the women would come in long colorful summer dresses and wearing earrings and bracelets. I loved to walk among them stealthily, because I didn't want them to notice me, and to listen to their talk and to hear the ice clink in the tall glasses filled with bourbon or Scotch and to watch the men and women smoke cigarettes, especially the women, leaving bright red lipstick marks on their blazing white cigarettes. When they put them out, they were crushed, with crimson mouthprints on the stub. Later, when I examined the hills of stubs in the ashtrays, I could tell whether a woman smoked the cigarette or a man. If there was an ocean breeze, it would move the women's summer skirts one way or another slightly from time to time. There was much laughter and the voices were mixed with masculine roars and female shrieks of recognition.

My mother had her hands full. Not just with the work of the house, but with my grandmother who came in May with her two black servants, with her expectations, and with her tacit judgment. We were rowdy kids, going outdoors and indoors all day long. The two of us were boys who very much acted like boys. I remember seeing my grandmother—whom I adored—standing by a door looking on stonily at me and my mother as my mother tried to stop me from destroying something in that house, in my grandmother's house. My eye just caught a glimpse of that look from my grandmother. It was cold, and biding.

Then there came a time when I would begin to see my mother changed. This was usually in the evening when she was in a pretty dress waiting for my father to come home from work. He began to come home later and later. And my mother started drinking. I saw her drink, and my father, too, but that was at parties on the summer porch. "Everyone drank back then," my mother said later. But then my mother started to change in the evenings. She would smile inappropriately. I didn't recognize that smile. It came from nowhere. Her head would jerk toward me if I called her. Her talk was saccharine and strange. She was not anyone I knew.

"Hon – nee," she would say, her face blurry.

"Yes, Mommy."

"Time for you to skeediddle-daddle."

"Mommy, don't say that."

"Why not, Sugarplum?"

"No, I don't like it."

"Skeediddle-daddle," she said, like an infant just learning a new word and pleased with it. She said it again. Her silk dress rustled as she gestured widely.

"No, Mommy, don't say it."

She slurred the word, saying it again. Come back, Mommy! I thought. Don't leave. Come back.

She didn't come back. Whatever it was that broke her finally, I don't know, but it broke her for good. She started drinking and didn't stop. My father's responsibility in all this? My mother's? My sister and I have talked about this for years, and we're not certain where and how to apportion the blame, as if that would be any help to anyone now. My father was not a good husband. He wasn't around much, and he was not very loving. He could be cruel and verbally sadistic to my sister and brother and to me. My mother was incapable of cruelty. She never said a malicious word in her life. If she said anything negative about someone, it was to protect herself, or it was really a howl of pain.

When we were talking about this years later on the phone, she in Florida, I in New York, I confronted her, "When Dad was cruel or violent to me, you didn't intervene."

"No, not much. Well, yes, I did. I hustled you out of there."

She paused.

"When you were little, he put ice down your back just to see you run around. I'll never forget that till the day I die. My mother was visiting. She thought he was crazy."

"Did I cry?"

"No. But you had such a look of confusion on your face. You didn't understand. My mother was so angry with him."

When I heard this, heard what he'd done, my heart went out to that little boy. But there was worse to come. I told my mother I was worried I would be cruel toward my own child in a burst of frustration.

"I know you're an innately sweet person," she said to me. "And a generous person."

Oh, God, Mommy, I hope so. Sometimes I wonder. But one thing I know for certain. I've never been cruel to my daughter. I've never made her feel unworthy.

She said about my father, "I found out he could be a hypocrite. He could be a real Southern gentleman. But he had two sides to his personality. He succeeded in crushing me. He wanted to grind his heel into people."

Then she shocked me.

"He hit me," she said calmly.

"*What?*"

"I had a big black eye. Dr. Mullen guessed." Dr. Mullen was her pediatrician.

"Why did he do it?"

"I don't know. I was nagging him about an apartment, I think."

"When was this?"

"Well, I still had Dr. Mullen, so you must have been young."

But what use is this? What use is this post-mortem? Later, I heard talk of an affair my father had had. Somebody even said my mother had one as well. The only thing that mattered to me was that sometime in the late 1950s I lost my mother, the mother I had known, and I never got her back again. I got someone else.

The divorce from my father in 1957 exploded our family's life into thousands of glassy fragments. My mother packed us up—my brother, sister and me—and took us far north to Michigan, to a land that was strange and hostile. It was cold, with people who did not think or act or talk like us, and around whom we felt outcasts. That's when the heavy drinking began, when she became a full-fledged alcoholic. If you've lived it, you know it.

She took us to St. Clair, Michigan. She went there because her sister, Dottie, her only sibling, lived there. She had no place else to go. I'm sure she didn't want to go back to Dayton and to the humiliation of living with her parents. St. Clair was a small town about two hours north of Detroit where many auto executives went to retire because of the hilly views of the wide, swift St. Clair River. It was also a small rural town, with girls who got pregnant at fifteen out of stark boredom and who were grandmothers in their thirties. It was a petty, gossipy, intolerant town. We moved from house to house, finally settling in a small, one-story, cheerless place far from the river. Every once in a while I would wonder what had happened to me. God knows, my mother must have, too. We had known salt water, sun, honeysuckle- and gardenia-scented air and Tidewater accents. She took us to a place that was gray with silty heavy water; to strange-cadenced accents; and to a cold that began in August and seeped into your bones and stayed there until the following July. I remember having to put on a thick flannel shirt the first day of school in early September.

The drinking. The drinking. It ruined everything. I didn't know who I was speaking to anymore. My mother was gone. She wasn't there anymore. Someone else had come in and was living there. Nothing Topsy did was familiar. Nothing she said sounded like her. Her face became blurry and indistinct. She gained weight. She often shrugged her shoulders for no reason and made strange sounds that seemed to signify a response to someone or something we couldn't see. She became hyper-sentimental, easily wounded, desperately sad, hurt, hurt, hurt. She would look at us with beseeching eyes and smile crookedly, or she would ignore us, sitting on the couch, staring. She wasn't a mother anymore. She was hardly a woman—not what I knew to be a woman. She became a drinker in her nightgown, getting fatter and more and more lost.

What could we do? We were entitled to an adolescence, with the normal confusion and exploding egos, but we didn't get it. Never got it. She usurped it. She stole it. We weren't allowed to have problems that needed attending, or worries, or doubts, or rebellions. Her problems and sadnesses were the only problems and sadnesses allowed in that house. If we dared to bring up some anxiety we had, she would say, "Don't you love me?" Or, if we hinted that we might be unhappy, she challenged us, "Do you love your father more than you love me?"

"No, Mom, no!"

"You do!" And she would begin crying.

"Mom, don't cry. Please!"

"You don't know how much I love you!" Her eyes would be brimming with tears, and she would sit there in her old nightgown, legs slightly spread, reaching for a Kleenex. "You never will."

Once, after we had prodded her relentlessly about doing something with her life—"Mom, you were a newspaper woman! You had your own column! You can get a job!"—she did get a job with a newspaper in Port Huron, a bigger town not far from St. Clair. We were thrilled. We were hopeful. She might find herself again. We might get her back.

It didn't last. One day we returned home from school to find her on the couch in her nightgown.

"What happened, Mom? Why aren't you at the newspaper?"

"Oh, it didn't work out," she said, waving an absent hand.

"But..."

"I don't want to talk about it now."

About the drinking, she said to me later, "I wasn't always a drunk. I didn't start to drink until you were six or seven."

I pushed my own needs aside. I tended her. I gave my adolescence away. I kept quiet, for fear of saying anything that she might interpret as not loving her. I went off to a boarding school about two hours from St. Clair. I was miserable there, but better that than stay at home in that soul-crushing town with her. She would come to visit me. She was usually disheveled, blurry. She had that inappropriate smile. Two or three times she walked in and said, "I just got into an accident. A very bad car accident." It seemed so unreal. I was never sure she was telling the truth. Why is it she always came to me in need? What could I say, or do? Why did she have to come drunk to school, in front of my friends?

My mother never remarried. She did have affairs and romances. A divorced woman in that time was considered an immoral woman. That seems hard to believe now, but I assure you it's true. Especially in a small town. She had to bear that stigma. That, and the lack of money, and the loss of my father's love, all that and more must have been so hard for her. How much can one person bear? This was an insupportable time to be a divorced woman. Divorce already brings with it so much pain and shame and a deep sense of failure. Add to that the mores of the 1950s, before the Women's Movement, before the great shift in law and sentiment, and you have the burden my mother carried each and every day—and in that godforsaken town. I don't see how she did it. Well, she reached for the bottle. I know about that. I do now. I've reached for it plenty of times myself. I am so much like her, weak and strong.

As for lovers, I remember once getting up in the night—I would have been about thirteen—and coming downstairs. I think there was music playing too loud. I saw her with a man I didn't know, her blouse unbuttoned, her bra visible and askew. Oh no! Don't! I thought. Then she looked down and saw herself exposed and quickly masked the whiteness with her hand.

There was one constant man, his name was Alan, an Englishman who was in love with my mother and would have married her. He was a kind, soft-spoken man, but we children ridiculed his ways. My mother I don't think could or would have married anyone after my father. Anyway, she never did.

I went off to the University of Michigan. My brother went to Tufts. My sister went to the University of Missouri. I wish we had been better help to one another. We were in our own separate worlds, though, trying to survive, trying to stay afloat.

Then, in the early 1970s, she moved to New York City. That saved her life. We—her children—were gone. We had graduated from college and were leading our own lives. Even though her sister Dottie still lived in St. Clair, Topsy realized one day that staying in that place was suicide. She said to me later, "I woke up one morning, and I saw that I was killing myself." She didn't know anyone in New York, but at least her old Wheaton roommate, Elsa—who had introduced her to my father—lived nearby in Greenwich, Connecticut. So in the early 1970s, Topsy moved to New York and found an apartment at 55th Street, just east of First Avenue. New York gave her what St. Clair never did, or could—dignity. And a zest for life. New York treats everyone with the same indifference, and that is a precious gift. For all its faults, and I know most of them now, having lived there for thirty years, it is the least judgmental place I know. Whatever personal falls you may have taken, or missteps, they are not important or relevant here. New York accepts you, no questions asked. Where else can you find that?

My mother went from a town that was endlessly dull and prying to one that is endlessly stimulating and indifferent. "All I have to do is walk from my apartment to Bloomingdale's, and I'm thoroughly entertained," she once said. This is a city that did not care or even want to know if she was divorced, or if she drank too much, or if she was overweight, if she didn't speak that often to her children, or if she didn't have much money. It says, look, you belong here just as much as the next person. If you can handle me, if you can manage the rent, you're welcome. My mother had no more child support money, since we were adults now. So she had to work. She got a job as a secretary at an insurance agency. She didn't like that, but she needed the money. Still, she was happy in New York. I saw her transformed. I will always be grateful to New York for that.

    I got her back. And she, Wheaton. She started reconnecting with the women she went to school with so many years ago. She saw Elsa and her husband often. She began going to reunions, and seeing once again those women who had played such a part in her life in that place that meant so much to her. I would meet some of these women later when they came to New York to shop and to drop by my mother's apartment. Years later, after my mother died, I tried to find out more about her four years at Wheaton. I called up the alumni office to see what they could send me about her. They had very little about her. They directed me to the library, and the woman in charge of archives xeroxed my mother's yearbook photograph and sent it to me. When I looked at it for the first time, I gasped at her loveliness. She's so young, not a flaw on her face. Shimmering.

    This is how I prefer to think of her, when she was beautiful and smart and young. I prefer to think of her when she was her happiest, those years at Wheaton. I can picture it. Perhaps she's just gone out riding—she was on the school equestrian team—and when she comes back to the dorm she is met by a razzing and by held noses because of the stable smell she brings with her. (An old Wheaton chum mentioned that fondly in her eulogy.) Or maybe it's on a white winter's day, and she and Elsa go out skating in the afternoon. The sharp air brings her face alive and she returns invigorated to a warm room and brisk chocolate. Casting off the cold, she sits and begins to read a book, her bright eyes narrowed and alive, her mind curious. She turns the pages, intent, absently brushing aside a strand of her rich brown hair as she reads, not regarding time or fatigue or hunger.